...-hole Games

NATURALITY

LIVING ACCORDING TO OUR NATURE, WALKING OUR OWN PATH

by Jivasu

NEITHER RELIGIOUS NOR SPIRITUAL BUT NATURAL

FriesenPress

Suite 300 - 990 Fort St
Victoria, BC, V8V 3K2
Canada

www.friesenpress.com

First Edition — 2016

All non-attributed quotes are by the author.

Cover painting by Shipra

ISBN
978-1-4602-8282-3 (Hardcover)
978-1-4602-8283-0 (Paperback)
978-1-4602-8284-7 (eBook)

1. BODY, MIND & SPIRIT

Distributed to the trade by The Ingram Book Company

DEDICATION

FOUR PILLARS OF MY LIFE

Karen – my wife, whose all-embracing love paved the path for my Naturality journey

Ammaji – my grandmother, who sowed the seeds of spirituality through her many stories

Papaji – my father, whose patient and calm guidance prevented me from drowning in my own chaos

Mummyji – my mother, who taught me how to care and serve with love

FOUR SAGES WHO INSPIRED ME

Sri Aurobindo and Mother – my first inspiration for my adventure of consciousness. Their ideas and realization of consciousness in matter and body was revolutionary. They were the first ones to articulate integral yoga and spirituality

J. Krishnamurti – who inspired me to walk alone without a guru and to question authority

U. G. Krishnamurti – who brought biology and body to the forefront of liberation

TWO SAGES WHO TAUGHT ME BY THEIR BODILESS PRESENCE

Shirdi Sai Baba and Swami Chidananda Saraswati of Sivananda Ashram, Rishikesh, India

FOUR GREAT TEACHERS AND PHILOSOPHERS FROM WHOM I LEARNED

Osho – His lucid and joyful words helped me to articulate my own experiences and thoughts with flow and celebration. He is a great singer of spirituality.

Ernest Becker – His writings on death affirmed my insights that the fear of death of the ego is the core problem of humans.

Antonio Damasio – His neuropsychological research about emotions and self helped me to connect Naturality insights with the brain.

Ken Wilber – Through the writings of Ken Wilber, Sri Aurobindo's Integral Yoga became more clear and contemporary

CONTENTS

NATURALITY

(SAHAJTA)

LIVING ACCORDING TO OUR NATURE, WALKING OUR OWN PATH

INTRODUCTION

We have now entered an era in which faith-based paths no longer have the ability to quench our inner thirst. We must find a way where faith affirms reason and reason guides our faith.

Truth remains the same, but its interpretations differ according to the time period and cultural context. In order to stay contemporary, we must constantly reinterpret the Truth. The modern era urgently needs such a reinterpretation, because for the first time in human history, a world culture based on reason, science, academic education, material well-being and the rights of the individual is emerging.

As the old faiths are fading, many sense a void in their lives and are searching for new paths to guide them through the emptiness. There is a keen interest in self-inquiry and a yearning for a self-knowledge that connects us to our daily lives.

Our response to this aspiration of the nascent world culture is to offer the teachings of Naturality as educational tools, rather than as religious or spiritual beliefs and dogmas. Although these teachings are grounded in reason and science, there is a clear acknowledgement that both feelings and faith provide the essential energy and passion required to walk the path of Naturality.

Naturality programs are based on the following principles:

- Self-Care and Care of Others
- Self-Inquiry, Self-Knowledge and Self-Expression as processes on the path
- Integration of Evolution, Brain Science, Psychology and Physics as an understanding of the wholeness and sacredness of existence

Naturality bridges the gap between the nature within and the nature without; the wisdom of the ancients and the knowledge of the new; the individual and the universal. Also, it affirms the student-teacher dialogue in lieu of the guru-disciple relationship.

This book, *Naturality*, explores the causes and consequences of separation from our innate nature, as well as the process by which an individual can re-integrate with that nature.

SEVEN FEATURES OF NATURALITY

1. Fear of non-existence of the ego is the core problem of humans.
2. Naturality is not a goal but the process, and each point in the process is Naturality. It's in the beginning, it's is in the middle, it's in the end.
3. A healthy ego is the first milestone of Naturality.
4. Biology and body are the underpinning of all experiences on Naturality's path.
5. Naturality is education, and education means bringing forth what is already there within a person.
6. Naturality teachings are like scaffolding, helping to build our life and live it fully. Once life is built, the scaffolding should be discarded.
7. The teacher is the guide and not the authority on the path of Naturality.

Chapter 1

WHAT IS NATURALITY?

We are born from nature, sustained by nature and eventually return to nature. Yet somehow, we are separated from that very nature, both within and without. The seeds of this alienation are sown early in childhood. Young children have to depend on family, society and culture for survival and development. In this process, they are conditioned and molded by traditions, rules and customs. This is clearly necessary, because the child's brain is too immature to comprehend either the natural or the cultural world. A child not only needs physical shelter but also a sense of psychological safety, which is provided by family, culture and tradition.

This social conditioning forms the self or ego, which is needed in order to live in the world. However, there comes a time when such conditioning outlives its usefulness. If we are not able to go beyond it, it becomes a prison. We become alienated from our own nature and the world around us. This leads to conflict and discontent within ourselves, which manifests as violence and destruction. Because we can't ever be fully conditioned, we consciously or subconsciously remain on a quest for something more. We feel empty within and try to fill the void by accumulating wealth, power and knowledge. However, our thirst is not quenched. In fact, it becomes more intense as we learn more about ourselves.

Naturality is the process of understanding the cause of this fear, conflict and discontent. Naturality is also the process of understanding how to free ourselves from this prison. Because the problem is caused by inner factors, the solution has to be sought from within. External teachers can help in the beginning as guides, but they can't take us to the desired destination. We have to become our own teachers, open the book of life, investigate and find the answers on our own, like scientists. No one can provide us with the answers to our existential problems.

These problems and their solutions are not metaphysical, religious or spiritual in nature. They are connected with our biology. It is through our brain and the body that our ego, self and soul are experienced and expressed. In order to walk the path of Naturality, we must reconnect with our body and brain.

On the expansive ground of the universe, human life is like a tree. The body is the root, the brain is the trunk, the emotions are the branches and the intellect and thoughts are the leaves, flowers and fruits. If we only acquaint ourselves with the fruits, flowers and leaves, we will never know the whole tree.

As we start discovering our innate nature and the tree of life, a transformation that will break our conditioning will occur. Freedom from conditioning will allow us to fully express ourselves in the world and to live according to our own nature. We will live effortlessly in a state of becoming and being. In such a state, we become part of the "full life," in which stillness roars with energy, peace meets with passion and living and dying are two dimensions of a boundless existence.

On the path of Naturality, the body's inner rhythm regulates sleep, exercise, eating and sex. The flow of emotions and feelings take care of relationships and bonds (emotional intelligence), while reason and thought provide protection and structure (cognitive or intellectual intelligence). Living becomes as natural as a river flowing freely through a valley.

NATURALITY

Naturality is a derivation from the Latin, *Natura,* meaning "innate nature". In Sanskrit, the word Naturality can be translated to *Sahajta,* itself derived from the *Sahaja* – (*Saha* / with; *Ja*/born). The word *Sahaja* means "that with which we are born"—and we are born with our innate nature. Naturality embraces life's underlying harmony and flow. Even that which we consider artificial or abnormal still contains a fragment of the natural. Thus, Naturality encompasses belief in God as well as atheism, materialism and spirituality, science and religion, the organic and the artificial, health and disease, living and dying. These may seem to be opposites but they are all part of the same ever-flowing movement of life.

Biologically, our genetic makeup or genes determine our nature. This includes our physical body, emotions and thoughts. Genes are surrounded by epigenetic material, which regulates how genes will express themselves. This is further influenced by the biological and cultural environment in which we live. This means that all aspects of nature play a role in the moulding of a person's nature. The person, the world and the universe are all part of a single movement. Nature exists partly at the macro level, which is experienced by the senses. Nature also exists on a micro level, which cannot be experienced directly by the senses. This subtle, micro level of Nature is called the "quantum" reality by scientists. But the quantum realm is not the whole story of existence. There is a realm beyond quantum which can't be captured by the senses or science because it's beyond time and space and so remains unknowable. It can only be experienced directly when all conditioning, concepts, definitions and teachings come to a total and complete end.

Our physical body, emotions and thoughts are connected and influenced by a much larger biological reality then we can comprehend. Here "biological" means a living and conscious entity. It is like a vast ocean that we can never know in its entirety. However, a single drop from this ocean can quench our thirst. Naturality is the process of biological and psychological expansion, until all boundaries are broken and we are released into the boundless ocean of life.

RELIGION, SPIRITUALITY AND NATURALITY

At this point, it is important to make a distinction between religion, spirituality and naturality. The word religion comes from the Latin word *religare*, which means to "bind together." Religion is a powerful social force meant to unite people through a belief system, faith-based doctrines and a common code for inner and outer behavior. Thus, a religious person's consciousness is not individualized, but rather is rooted within a specific society and culture. Many religions are exclusive by nature and cannot accept other religions at an equal level.

In many contemporary societies, religion is fading in importance from people's lives. A scientific world view and the primacy of the individual over the collective have made traditional religious beliefs and practices less relevant. Yet we humans cannot live with an inner vacuum, and so as religion fades in a society, spirituality takes its place. Spirituality is based on personal faith and beliefs and includes specific practices. Through these practices and beliefs, a person experiences growth and the expansion of life. Unlike religion, spirituality is not used for social, cultural or political purposes. It is more individualistic, with a liberal view of humans and the natural world. However, spirituality can also be exclusive, as there are certain teachers, practices, beliefs and behaviors that are deemed superior to others. Spirituality is the first step to breaking the bonds of mass consciousness of religion and venturing into one's own nature.

In contrast to both religion and spirituality, Naturality is a process of accepting life in its totality, which encompasses fear and stillness, sorrow and joy, turmoil and peace. It is an effort to know one's own nature and the nature of the external world, two sides of the same reality. Naturality is non-moral in the sense that it doesn't differentiate between inner virtues and vices, as we perceive them in our mind. However, the person walking on the path of Naturality must behave in an ethical way, as this is essential to maintain order in a community or society. For example, a mother might punish her child because he or she is doing something inappropriate (external), but she does not judge her child within her own heart and mind (internal).

Naturality doesn't divide life into either the material or the spiritual. Theism and atheism, religion and spirituality are all recognized as part of the process of self-discovery. Any practice that helps us find our innate nature is beneficial—whether secular, religious or spiritual. The person walking the path of Naturality becomes a conscious observer of daily life, expanding his or her awareness of both the biological and psychological dimensions of life. During this process of expansion and observation, we discover innate physical and mental responses to food, exercise, sleep, people and places. By learning to follow these innate responses, a feeling of wellness is achieved. This process slowly brings us to a state where the non-essential falls away and we start living according to our innate nature.

When we study Naturality, we are challenged to investigate the causes of fear, conflict and discontentment in the world. We are encouraged to find solutions that honor our own nature and environment so we can live in a state of peace, passion and bliss. The process of walking the path of Naturality is never-ending. There is no final destination, because arrival at any point becomes the beginning of another journey. Life is boundless.

The philosophy of Naturality emphasized the importance of an individual's quest for inner truth, rather than merely following the direction of a prophet, guru or teacher. The word *guru* means "remover of darkness" and the word *teacher* means "one who points." Neither a teacher nor guru can reveal to us our innate nature. Instead, they can give valuable guidance on our journey towards discovering our own innate natures. But beyond a certain point, they become obstacles in the journey. Ultimately, we must find our own path, and then the teacher no longer has a role in the journey.

THREE STORIES TO UNDERSTAND NATURALITY

1. **When I feel hungry I eat**

   Bankei was a Japanese Zen master who was known for his simplicity. Once a learned man came to him and regaled him with stories about his teacher. He told Bankei that this man had miraculous powers. He could take a pen and write in the air and the words would appear as if they were written on a sheet of paper. The man then asked Bankei what kinds of miracles he could do. Bankei replied crisply, "We know only one miracle here . . . When I feel hungry I eat, and when I feel sleepy I sleep. Only this much . . ."

2. **I am what I am**

   A student came to the teacher and said, "I am relaxed and peaceful."

   "Throw away the relaxation and peace and meditate," replied the teacher.

   The student meditated and came back. "I discovered my soul."

   "Throw away the soul and meditate."

   The student meditated and met with the teacher: "I experienced Nirvana."

   "Throw away the Nirvana and meditate."

   The student didn't return. The teacher found him peacefully dancing in the marketplace.

   "What happened to you?" he asked.

   The student replied, "*I am what I am, Natural . . .*"

3. Living like a butterfly is liberation

"How do I find liberation?" asked a student from his teacher.

"Go into the forest and follow the *life of a butterfly*," replied the teacher.

After a month of living in the forest with butterflies, the student returned.

He understood the meaning of liberation. Living according to our nature is liberation.

Chapter 2

AWARENESS OF DEATH AND LIFE: THE FORMATION OF EGO

SELF-AWARENESS: THE JOY AND SORROW OF EVOLUTION

As human beings, we have developed a remarkable capacity for self-awareness and self-reflection, which brings us the delight and joy of life. Although this self-awareness is present in some animals such as dolphins, chimpanzees and elephants, in humans it is expansive, extending into the remote past and into the distant future. We are aware not only of our personal past but that of our country, race or religion. We can also speculate about our future. By virtue of self-awareness and self-reflection, we can connect our experiences in meaningful patterns, making us the most creative living beings on earth. Our capacity for self-reflection gives us the ability to restrain emotional impulses and delay gratification. This gives us control over ourselves so that we can plan for a better, more comfortable future.

However, this self-awareness comes at a cost. We are not only conscious of life and its beauty, but also of death. Individually and collectively, the core challenge for all human beings is the fear of death. But it is not physical death that haunts us, but the certainty of non-existence of our consciousness. This fills us with fear and we spend our lives trying to escape and transcend this reality.

FORMATION OF THE EGO

The fear of death begins around the age of three, when a child becomes self-conscious. This is also the beginning of conscious memory. Although memories begin to form before the age of three, they are buried deep within the subconscious mind. A child is not only frightened by the mystery of death, but also by the complexity of life. A child's brain is not developed enough to comprehend the turbulent and unpredictable nature of life or the intricacies of culture.

The fear of death forces a child to reach out to parents and caretakers for shelter, safety and comfort. Protection is provided through the love of the family, as well as through beliefs and mythology around the protective powers of forces such as God, country, race, morality, traditions and knowledge. These stories become a part of a child's belief system, which firmly roots him or her into the family, culture and society. This is the formational stage of the ego or self, a necessity for the healthy development of a child.

We live in a vast universe, most of which is unknown to us. A core function of the ego is to take the nameless and formless incomprehensible truth and its myriad expressions and bring them into the field of the known. It's done by giving names and symbols to the nameless and formless. This gives us a sense of control over that which is unknown. For example, we may label the unknown as "God." By naming the unknown, we feel that we regain a measure of control through ritual, worship and prayer. Through the use of symbols, we try to manipulate that which is beyond our grasp. Human history is replete with symbols created in order to deal with the unpredictable forces of nature, as well as life and death. Of them all, God has emerged as the supreme symbol used and abused throughout history.

The ego is a social and cultural construct about oneself and the world. It is a concept borrowed from family and culture and is not uniquely our own. It is based on a belief system rather than on facts. However, the ego provides relief from the fear of death and life by creating a symbolic and mythical world where things don't die. It acts as a filter, allowing in only a bearable amount of experience of about life and death. This filtering is essential for psychological survival. Many children who suffer from anxiety, depression, emotional disregulation and other mental illnesses, have not developed a strong ego. An inadequately developed ego allows an overwhelming amount of information to flood into the brain, which has a devastating impact on the child's emotional and physical well-being. Also, early damage of the ego by trauma can create lifelong wounds not easily healed even if the person becomes a well-adjusted adult in society.

We see then, that the ego plays an important role in creating a healthy person. Without a well-established ego, we feel lost and frightened by the immensity of the world and the stark realities of life and death. If we try to deny the ego as part of our spiritual quest, we are risking serious emotional trauma. Instead, we must begin by ensuring that our foundations are sound by developing a healthy ego before we attempt to go beyond the ego.

THE EGO AND THE ILLUSION OF IMMORTALITY

The core challenge facing humans is the fear of death and of life—however, it is not so much the fact of physical death that frightens us, but rather the fear of the death of the ego which represents self-awareness. We cannot bear to think that after we die, nothing at all will remain of us. To address this deep-rooted problem, the ego creates the world of names and forms, time and space. We can't live with the nameless and formless, because the unknown brings fear.

Through the ego, we change the unknown into symbols, concepts and definitions. By this process of categorizing and organizing our world, we feel a sense of relief from fear.

Another protective function of the ego is that it creates a mental time and space, and this artificial world imparts a sense of vicarious immortality. Ego as "I" becomes a reference point that stands in the present. Whatever has happened becomes the past, and what hasn't yet happened is the future. Ego creates an endless future and lives in it because in an endless future, time never ends and life continues. In this way, the ego imparts a sense of immortality. Heaven, hell, the spirit world and rebirth are all creations of the ego's immortality drive. The ego's illusory immortality is also achieved through one's children, a legacy, a mention in history, charity, monuments, works of art, scientific achievements, and in many other ways.

Finally, let's consider the concept of *mental space*. Mental space is the psychological distance between people, nations and religions that causes conflict in the world. It is responsible for the human hostility towards nature and also the conflict within a person when the various parts of the ego are not in harmony with each other. The experience of anger and guilt are the result of such inner conflict. Mental space causes conflict, and this conflict brings decay and death within the individual and also in the world. Through the ego, we long to transcend this mental space to achieve a sense of immortality. We begin to universalize our perspective on the world through cultivating a sense of love and compassion. By this expanded perception, the ego feels connected to others around the world, even those in who live in different circumstances or hold different beliefs. This universalization of perspective creates a wonderful sense of love towards others. Yet the ego still remains alive and intact. The only difference is that the ego has now expanded and there is an illusory sense that this expansion is boundless transcendence.

THE PRISON OF THE EGO

Giving a name and form helps us to acquire knowledge about the laws of nature. We can then use this knowledge to improve our quality of life and prolong our survival. However, in the process of naming the unknown, life becomes confined to symbols and its free movement is restricted by our own rigid concepts. Symbols can only give us a narrow and limited experience of living rather than a joyful and boundless life.

The prison created by the ego also causes us to lose touch with our own innate nature. This process begins in the early years of human life, as the child is gradually molded by an ego manufactured by culture. A point comes when the child loses contact with his or her innate nature. However, this disconnection is never complete nor is this surrender ever total. The flame of innate nature burns brightly deep within.

If we were completely ignorant of our innate nature, we would live without conflict. However, our innate nature is dynamic and constantly sends signals of its presence. We may ignore it in order to maintain a comfortable existence within society, but we live a fragmented life plagued by a persistent conflict between our innate nature and the ego. It is the struggle between what is and what should be. The ego protects us but it also takes away the full experience of who we are.

This fragmented life can lead to a persistent state of alienation, conflict and discontent. It takes away the natural joy of life. As a result, we struggle with a deep sense of frustration, and we try to assuage that frustration by the pursuit of material goods, power, money, food, sex, or drugs. The endless pursuit of material goods results in ever-increasing consumption of the world's resources. Such lifestyles are ultimately unsustainable, and lead inevitably to environmental destruction. We can depict the sequence of events as a chain of interdependent factors, shown below.

SEVEN INTERDEPENDENT FACTORS BEHIND HUMAN PROBLEMS

Emergence of self-awareness

Fear of living and dying

Formation of ego, to provide a sense of safety and immortality

Alienation, conflict and discontent

Decline in pleasure and well-being

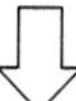

Consumption of power, wealth, food, sex,
drugs, knowledge for **pleasure**

Environmental destruction

Scientists worldwide are writing about the devastating effects of a consumer lifestyle on the environment. This is perhaps the greatest challenge facing human beings today. Scientists and politicians have proposed many solutions. Yet we can never solve the environmental crisis through technological fixes, laws or regulations alone. Instead, we must address the underlying issue, which is the fundamental discontent that we face when we are alienated from our true selves.

We are aware that something is missing from our lives—something precious and unique. Only when we are able to feel a sense of wholeness and fulfillment will we stop the endless cycle of craving and consumption.

Chapter 3

PRAKIRTI: KNOWING OUR INNATE NATURE

"The most beautiful book to study is the book of our life"

Understanding our innate nature as well as learning about the body's energy centres (chakras) is the foundation of Naturality. With this core of understanding, we can learn from diverse sources and traditions without confusion. We can learn from a guru and teacher but we should not become dependent on them. By exploring our own nature we will discover the teacher and guru within—our source of insight and wisdom. By understanding the energy centres or chakras, we learn about the world and nature. This will give us a clear understanding of evolution and involution, from both a biological and psychological perspective.

In this chapter, we will focus on the first of these two foundational ideas: our innate nature. We are each born with a unique nature, which expresses itself in our mind-body constitution or personality. The mind and body are two expressions of the same intelligence and orient us in the world.

Innate nature is formed through the combination of three influences:

1. Genes from parents (genetics)
2. Influence of ancestors, family members and environment, which modifies the genetic expression in an individual (epigenetics)
3. Karmas (memories) from past lives (NOTE: A belief in rebirth is not necessary in order to understand this concept. We could also say that memories and tendencies are encoded in one's genes.)

As we explored in the previous chapter, the emergence of the ego or self, conditioned by culture, buries our innate nature deep within our being. However, the ego can't suppress our natural self entirely, which results in a mind-body conflict and a lack of well-being. Such an imbalance disturbs the rhythms of life, including sleep, appetite and sex, resulting in a lack of fulfillment and natural pleasure in life. We then begin to search for pleasure in external sources, which can lead to dependence and addiction. Yet underneath the ego, our innate nature remains alive and intact. The recovery of our innate nature requires self-observation and diligent practice. As we become more closely in touch with our innate nature, we can feel something deep and true beginning to emerge. If we are allowed to blossom fully, wholeness and well-being is experienced.

INNATE NATURE: INSIGHTS FROM AYURVEDA

The ancient Indian system of Ayurveda is more than a system of healing. The word *Ayurveda* means "knowledge of life," and traditionally, the Ayurvedic physician would advise his patients about many aspects of their lives. He would prescribe not only herbal medicines, but also suggest lifestyle changes. The philosophy underlying Ayurveda provides some fascinating insights into the differences between various personality types and temperaments. This ancient system of knowledge can be used as a tool to learn about one's innate nature. Innate nature means the mind-body personality with which we are born.

According to Ayurvedic philosophy, we can also learn about innate nature through the concept of the three *doshas* or mind-body personalities: Vata (Wind), Pitta (Fire) and Kapha (Earth). The word *dosha* comes from *dus*, which is related to the English prefix "dys,", meaning flawed. One's constitution or personality is called a *dosha* because it can be easily disturbed by external and internal factors.

Knowing our mind-body personality provides a preliminary concept of our unique innate nature. To know one's nature requires observation as well as knowledge of the body's physical features, emotional responses, and patterns of thought. This knowledge can then be refined and expanded through ongoing and spontaneous self-observation. In other words, to know our innate nature means opening the book of our life and studying it.

Besides the concept of the three doshas, we must also understand the concept of the five elements. It is important to realize that we are speaking here in a metaphorical way rather than in a strictly scientific way. We are not discussing a chemical analysis of matter, nor discussing the periodic table of the elements. Rather, we are drawing on ancient concepts and ideas about the world that have proved useful over the centuries. Sages in the Indian Ayurvedic tradition considered that the world was composed of five essential elements: earth, water, fire, air and space. These elements can be used to describe not only the physical world around us, but also the human body and mind. Looking more closely at the human body, Ayurvedic sages described how various combinations of the elements form unique bodily constitutions, or temperaments. So the elements form both the individual (microcosm) and the universal (macrocosm) nature. These elements can be experienced through somatic sensations—in other words, through feelings. As we learn more about our individual constitutions, we can also learn to live in a more relaxed and healthy manner in the world.

In the following section, the five elements will be described, along with the corresponding constitution. It's important to note that nobody's constitution is composed of only one type; we all have a blend of various elements that make up our unique nature. But usually one constitution is predominant. By learning about the underlying constitutional types, we can begin to balance our constitution through making deliberate changes in our lifestyle.

THE FIVE ELEMENTS

1. The first element is **Earth and is felt as solidity**. It resides in the sacral area where the root energy centre or chakra is located. It spreads from here to the whole mind-body. Earth is solid, stable, cool and calm. It roots and nurtures. All smells emerge from the earth so it is connected with our sense of smell and the nose.

2. The second element is **Water and is felt as fluidity**. Water resides close to the pubic bone in front of the body where the bladder and second or sex centre of energy is located. It spreads from here to the whole mind-body. Water is lighter than earth and is fluid, cool, and calm. Without water, taste cannot be experienced. Therefore, water is connected with our sense of taste and the tongue.

3. The third element is **Fire and is felt as energetic and passionate movement**. Fire resides at the naval point where the solar centre of energy or chakra is located and spreads from there to the whole mind-body. Fire moves quickly. It is lighter than water and it is hot, dry and passionate. Fire produces light and

without light we cannot see. Therefore, fire is connected with our sense of vision and the eye.

4. The fourth element is **Air and is felt as lightness and quick movement.** Air resides in the middle of the chest where the heart centre of energy or chakra is located and spreads from there to the whole mind-body. Air is lighter than fire. It is ever moving, cool, dry, unstable and connected to our sense of touch and the skin.

5. The fifth element is **Space and is felt as expansiveness**. Space resides at the root of the neck where the throat center of energy or chakra is located and spreads from here to the whole mind-body. In space all other elements live and grow. Space is the lightest, coldest element and is present everywhere simultaneously because of its infinite movement. Without space, sound cannot travel and therefore, space is connected with hearing and the ear.

INNATE NATURE OR PRAKIRTI

When the five elements combine, three mind-body personalities, Doshas or constitutions emerge. The various combinations of these personalities shape the unique nature of each human being.

When earth and water elements combine, the **Earth personality** is born. The parasympathetic nervous system is more active in this personality.

When water and fire elements combine, the **Fire personality** is born. This personality is a combination of the sympathetic and parasympathetic nervous systems.

When the air and space elements combine, the **Wind personality** is born. In this personality, the sympathetic nervous system is more active.

There is no pure personality or constitution—each individual has components of all the three main constitutions. However, in most people one constitution tends to dominate.

We can learn about our own unique constitutional blend by reflecting on a variety of physical and psychological characteristics. In the next section, each basic constitutional type will be described. By studying these descriptions, we can begin to identify characteristics that reflect our own mind and body. As we learn more and more about our inherent constitution, we can make changes to our lifestyle in order to balance the constitutional elements that may be causing ill-health.

THE CONSTITUTIONAL TYPES AND THE AUTONOMIC NERVOUS SYSTEM

The basic constitutional types were described by Ayurvedic scholars thousands of years ago. Using scientific terminology, we can make a linkage between the constitutional types and the human nervous system. The **autonomic nervous system** is responsible for survival and dynamic balance (homeostasis) of the body and brain. It does not need the conscious mind for its functioning. Emotions and feelings are intimately connected to the sympathetic and parasympathetic divisions of the autonomic nervous system.

The **sympathetic nervous system** is the emergency response system of the body and brain. It elicits the fight, flight or freeze reaction when faced with internal or external danger. It diverts blood from the skin, the digestive and reproductive organs to the heart, brain and muscles in order to prepare for action. The heart rate and blood pressure rise, the muscles tense, digestion and reproduction slow or shut down entirely and breathing becomes rapid and shallow. One feels nervous and tense.

Activation of the **parasympathetic nervous system** creates a state of rest and relaxation, the opposite of the sympathetic response.

Blood goes to the skin, digestive and reproductive organs. The muscles relax and the heart rate and blood pressure drop. One feels calm and grounded.

In some people, the sympathetic nervous system is more readily activated, while in other people it is parasympathetic nervous system that predominates. We can now make a linkage between the constitutional types and the autonomic nervous system.

THE THREE BASIC CONSTITUTIONAL TYPES

1. WIND OR SYMPATHETIC

Wind has air and space elements. It is the most unstable personality type, because of the presence of swiftly moving air in the expansiveness of space.

Body

People with a Wind-predominant constitution tend to be thin, with dry, cold skin.

Sleep: They are often restless sleepers, and have many dreams.

Eating: They may have an irregular appetite and poor digestion. Their weight may fluctuate rapidly.

Exercise: They can move rapidly, but they often have poor endurance.

Sex: Quick arousal and fall.

Mind

Emotion: Their predominant emotion is anxiety—they can be quite nervous and fearful.

Cognition: People with Wind-predominant constitutions tend to be highly creative, and ideas come easily to them. However, their thoughts may be unfocused, with frequently changing theories.

Memory: Their memory tends to be poor.

Relationships: Unless they find someone with a stable, warm constitution, Wind-predominant people may have unstable and frequent relationships.

Occupations: Artists, musicians, painters, writers and poets.

Unbalanced Wind

With an excess of movement of air in space, one may

- become restless, cold and exhausted
- experience a loss of appetite and weight with bowel disturbances
- develop low blood pressure, insomnia, headaches
- experience anxiety, panic attacks and chaotic thinking

How to maintain Wind in balance

Sleep: People with this constitution should try to ensure that they get a long sleep every night.

Eating: Three preferred tastes—sweet, salty and sour. Food should be accompanied with plenty of warm liquids.

Exercise: Ideally, exercise should be moderate and calming. Peaceful yoga, tai-chi and receptive meditation are best.

Relationships: If these people find someone with a stable, warm constitution, their relationship can be long-lasting and satisfying.

Emotional and cognitive: Because Wind people need to balance their creative and sometimes unstable thought patterns, they do well with people who tend towards methodical and logical thinking.

Work: People of Wind-predominant constitution should try to get into a type of work that is structured, in a stress-free, supportive environment.

2. FIRE OR INTERFACE OF PARASYMPATHETIC AND SYMPATHETIC

Fire has water and fire elements.

Body

People with a Fire-predominant constitution tend to be well-built, with ruddy and oily skin. Their body remains warm, and their gait is steady but impatient.

Sleep: They tend to sleep well, and have intense dreams.

Eating: Often, they have a strong appetite and good digestion. They are generally able to maintain a steady weight.

Exercise: They have good endurance and they usually enjoy physical activity.

Sex: Passionate and satisfying.

Mind

Emotion: People of Fire-predominant constitution tend to be energetic and passionate about what they do.

Cognition: They are good at making quick decisions and are action-oriented people. They tend to be persistent and focused in their behavior. They can be egotistical and opinionated.

Memory: Their memory tends to be sharp.

Relationships: People of Fire-predominant temperament are often able to form relationships quickly. However, for a happy and long-lasting relationship, they need to be matched with someone whose temperament is well suited—for example, someone of Earth temperament. Two people of Fire temperament may have difficulty sustaining a long-lasting, happy relationship.

Occupations: Fire-predominant people are often activists, political and business leaders, and pioneers.

Unbalanced Fire

As with any other constitution, there are negative consequences when Fire becomes unbalanced.

One may:

- become restless
- develop rashes and heartburn
- develop high blood pressure
- develop insomnia
- become irritable, revengeful and destructive
- develop excessive anger leading to depression.

How to maintain Fire in balance

Sleep: For people with a Fire-predominant constitution, a good sleep every night is essential.

Eating: There are three preferred tastes: bitter, astringent and sweet. These have pacifying and cooling qualities, which is helpful in balancing this constitution. Cold water and cooling foods are also helpful.

Exercise: These people should choose forms of exercise that are moderate and calming. For example, a relaxing form of yoga or tai-chi will help to calm them. Meditation practices such as mindfulness are well suited to people of this temperament.

Emotional and cognitive: Fire-predominant people should avoid confrontation with others, which will aggravate their fiery nature. They should set challenging goals for themselves, in which logical thinking and action are involved.

Work: These people have natural leadership qualities, and a work structure that allows them to use these skills will be satisfying.

3. EARTH OR PARASYMPATHETIC

Earth is formed by earth and water elements.

Body

People in whom earth is the dominant constitutional type tend to have a solid stocky build, a graceful slow walk, lustrous skin, hair and eyes and a cool body temperature.

Sleep: These individuals tend to sleep well, with few dreams.

Eating: Because they have an acute sense of smell and taste, most people with an earth-predominant constitution are fond of food. They easily gain weight and may have difficulty losing it.

Exercise: They tend to be slow to move but have good endurance.

Sex: Earth-predominant people tend to have a gradual sexual arousal but sustained passion.

Mind

Emotion: People of this constitutional type tend to be calm, caring and nurturing.

Cognition: They tend to ponder things deeply and make thoughtful decisions. They can be slow in making up their minds on an issue.

Memory: These people may take some time to remember but they retain memories for a long time.

Relationships: Because of the stable and accommodating nature of this constitutional type, these individuals tend to enjoy long-lasting relationships. They can partner with any other constitutional type.

Occupations: Earth-predominant people often tend to pursue careers in the health or education professions, where their calm and caring nature is a great blessing. They can also be found pursuing careers as athletes, negotiators and managers.

Unbalanced Earth

Each constitutional type has its own unique strengths as well as weaknesses. When the earth constitution becomes out of balance, various problems can arise. One may:

- become overweight or obese
- retain water in the body
- become lethargic and feel cold
- sleep excessively
- become emotionally static because of excess attachment
- feel withdrawn and depressed

How to balance the Earth constitution

After considering the physical and psychological characteristics of the Earth constitution, we can then formulate useful ways in which to balance the negative side of this constitutional type.

Sleep: People with an Earth constitution should take care not to over-sleep, which can create a feeling of sluggishness. They should also make it a habit to arise early in the morning.

Eating: These people must watch their diet closely, because of their tendency to gain weight. Dry, warm food in small quantities is best for them.

The best types of food are those that have drying and stimulating qualities—in particular, foods that taste bitter, astringent and pungent. Addition of these foods to the diet will help to balance this constitutional type.

Exercise: People with this constitution have great endurance and should exercise as much as they can. Those who wish to practice yoga should choose an active form of yoga, such as the Sun Salutation. Even meditation practices should be more active, such as walking meditation or chanting.

Emotional and cognitive: It is important for people with this constitution to constantly set new goals for themselves, in order to stimulate their minds and reach their highest potential.

Work: The best type of work for people with an Earth constitution is something that is both active and stimulating, involving the body. However, because of their innate stability, Earth people can thrive in a variety of work environments. They can tolerate even demanding schedules such as night shifts.

TABLE OF CONSTITUTIONAL TYPES

The following table summarizes the essential aspects of the various constitutional types. By studying this table, we can gain insight into our own unique constitutional type.

Qualities	*Sympathetic or Wind*	*Interface of sym. & parasym. or Fire*	*Parasympathetic or Earth*
BODY			
Build	Thin	Medium	Solid & stocky
Skin & Hair	Dry	Oily	Lustrous
Body Temperature	Cold, minimal sweating	Warm, profuse sweating	Cool, moderate sweating
Digestion	Poor	Good, intense appetite	Slow but good
Sexual Arousal	Quick arousal, quickly spent	Passionate sex life	Slow arousal but maintains
Exercise Endurance	Poor, exhausted quickly	Good	Can endure heavy exercise

Sleep & Dreams	Irregular sleep with many dreams	Good sleep with intense dreams	Good, deep with pleasant dreams
Pulse Rate	Around 80 or above/per min., may be irregular	60-80/per min., strong & stable	<60/per min, strong
MIND			
Memory	Poor	Sharp & good	Slow to remember but retain
Emotion	Fear	Excitement	Calmness
Thinking (cognition)	Plenty of superficial thoughts	Logical & precise	Slow & methodical
Stress Response	Anxiety/flight	Anger/fight	Freeze
Lifestyle	Irregular & erratic	Planned, busy	Steady, may be stuck in a rut
Vocation	Creative, artist	Leader, pioneer	Manager, caretaker
Natural Inclination	Original thinking & mystic	Action-taker	Loyal believer, follower

Chapter 4

THE CHAKRAS: WHEELS OF EVOLUTION AND INVOLUTION

In our study of conscious energy, we begin with Kundalini, a branch of yoga in the Indian tradition. *Kundalini* means "the coiled one." It has been called "the serpent power" because when dormant, it sits like a coiled serpent at the base of the spine. When it is awakened it is experienced as a column of energy curving upward from the base of the spine to the brain, like the shape of a hooded serpent. Energy moves upward through the spinal column, through the six primary centres, called the chakras.

Conscious energy (Kundalini) and the seven centres of conscious energy (Chakras) are metaphors for a variety of experiences brought about by the awakening of energy in the body and brain.

Even if we have not ourselves experienced that particular sensation of energy, the concept of Kundalini and the chakras can be very helpful as a metaphor to understand the evolution of human beings. Conscious energy refers to dormant energy in the body and nervous system at the base of the spine. A centre of conscious energy is called a *chakra*, which means "wheel" or "vortex." The chakras should not be thought of as anatomical or biological entities. Rather, we experience the chakras as a spiral or whirling movement of the energy through different regions of the brain and body, usually during deep meditation. The chakras are the windows through which the microcosm of the body and mind connect with the macrocosm of the universe. The macrocosm and the microcosm are formed by the same energy. Kundalini is also *Shakti*, or "force."

In the mind-body complex, each chakra is connected with a part of the brain. An activated chakra corresponds to a certain part of the brain, which is subsequently activated. In essence, the opening of the chakras means the opening of the brain. When the whole brain is activated and functioning, a union of the mind and body occurs. If this process continues, we develop an intimate connection between the mind-body and between the microcosm and macrocosm.

The chakras are milestones along the path of evolution and involution. All matter is energy and all energy is consciousness. However, all consciousness is not self-reflective and not all self-reflective consciousness is free from conditioning. Movement from non-reflective to self-reflective consciousness is evolution. The movement from a conditioned to an unconditioned self-reflective consciousness is involution.

When consciousness expands beyond the individual and becomes universal, it is involution. Such movement is like a fountain, which springs forth from the earth, goes up in a narrow stream, reaches its peak (evolution) and then comes down to the earth again as an expanded umbrella of water (involution).

Evolution is movement from lower to higher chakras. This movement from the first to the seventh chakra leads to integration of mind and body. It is the process of ascendance. Involution is movement from higher to the lower chakras, in which the individual becomes integrated with universal consciousness. It is the process of descent and expansion. For example, during evolution, the chakra opens partially but during involution it is fully functioning.

From a biological perspective, conscious energy is the total energy available to us. Part of this energy sustains the body and mind, while the rest is devoted to the process of individual evolution. The seven chakras are like seven brains in the human body. The seventh brain is not independent—it is an integration of the first six brains or chakras.

Social and cultural conditioning leads to chakra dormancy in which the chakras do not function at their optimal level or in harmony with one another. With the awakening of energy, the chakras become active and integrate with each other, leading to the fully functional individual. We'll explore this in one of the final chapters of this book. But before this, let's look at the general features of the chakras, and then take a more in-depth look at each individual chakra. We'll see that the chakras can be interpreted as a way of representing the human journey, from its earliest beginning to the highest peak of evolution. A study of Kundalini and the chakras give us unique insights about human nature and world in which we live.

GENERAL FEATURES OF THE CHAKRAS

The first two chakras are named the root (*Mooladhar*) and the sex (*Swadhisthan*) centres, and belong to matter and energy. They represent the body as well as the reptilian component of the brain, which is responsible for survival, sex and reproduction.

The third (solar or *Manipura*) and the fourth (heart or *Anahat*) chakras belong to emotions and feelings and represent the mammalian component in the brain. They are responsible for the six primary and many secondary emotions in human beings. Emotions help in promoting longer and better survival of the individual and the species.

The fifth chakra (throat or *Vishuddha*) belongs to logic, reason, language, and the anticipated future. It is represented by the neocortex, the uniquely human component of the brain. The fifth chakra helps humans to become powerful and to survive longer by inventing complex tools and technology. Also, the cognitive ability of self-reflection allows humans to learn from the past and to speculate about the future. With the activation of the fifth chakra, humans have the power to dominate all other living beings on earth. The first five chakras constitute the ego or the self.

The sixth chakra (third eye or *Ajna*) is the existential centre, where life and death face each other in stark opposition. Activation of the sixth chakra opens the subconscious, releasing a flood of fearful images, ideas and memories. One must face this fear in order to pass through the sixth chakra, into the seventh. At the seventh chakra, we shift into a different realm of consciousness, leaving the darkness and chaos of the sixth chakra behind us. Here we perceive universal consciousness for the first time.

To summarize, the higher Chakras are:

- more powerful—knowledge is power
- more easily accessible
- less difficult to open
- less dense
- less difficult to transform
- less important in the context of survival

Higher Chakras produce:

- more fear
- more choices
- more freedom
- more creativity

- more fluidity and less rigidity
- more survival
- more complexity
- more individuality

AN EXPLORATION OF EACH CHAKRA

THE FIRST CENTRE: ROOT CHAKRA (MOOLADHAR)

Rooting and Belonging; the Path of Matter

The path of Naturality begins with ascendance or evolution. The starting point for this journey is matter and energy. Matter and energy are the least conscious entities in the universe. Scientifically, they are the fundamental building blocks of the universe and all life emerges from them. Matter and energy are the foundations of human life, and they form the first two chakras, which constitute the physical body.

Although the first two chakras differ from one another in many ways, they have two features in common. First, they are composed of matter and energy, which are both interchangeable (the great insight of Einstein). Second, they form the physical and physiological, or the form and functional components of the body.

The first chakra is the chakra of death, of matter and of rooting and grounding. It is connected with the adrenal glands, which secrete the hormones that induce the fight or flight response to survive. Facing our own death can activate the root chakra. Here, survival is of paramount importance.

The first chakra is the root of the tree of life. This chakra is represented by the earth element because its strength holds the tree of life firmly to the ground. Human life is like a tree born from the seeds of two parents in the dark earth of the womb. From experiential point of view, the body is the root and trunk of the tree, the emotions and feelings are the branches and leaves, and thoughts are the flowers and fruits. Using the image of the brain, the spinal cord is the root, the brain stem is the stem, various nerves and plexuses are the branches and the cerebrum is the tree canopy. The root chakra is located at the end of the roots. This is at the level of the sacrum, near the lower end of backbone or in the perineum.

The energy of the first chakra is considered moon energy and is connected to the parasympathetic nervous system. Moon energy calms the body and mind and helps to ground and root us. We cannot face life's challenges without firm roots.

When we are grounded, we experience a sense of belonging, which is important for a healthy body and mind. A home is essential in order for us to thrive in this vast and complex world. The root chakra is connected with the reptilian component of the brain, which is responsible for all basic survival needs. The reptilian brain contains the cardiac and respiratory centres. This chakra communicates with our consciousness through sensations that are generated by the flow of energy through the nerves and cells.

The root chakra is also responsible for the expression of maleness and femaleness in a person. In addition, it determines the external appearance and sex of a person. In a man, the first chakra is masculine, the second is feminine, the third and fourth (as they form one functioning unit) are masculine, the fifth and sixth (again a functioning unit) are feminine, and the seventh has both masculine and feminine qualities. In a woman, this order is reversed.

This arrangement of gender expression has deep significance and indicates that none of us are pure male or female. We are a mixture of both. All too often, we are expected to behave strictly according to one gender or the other. Yet, on the path of Naturality, this rigid mold is broken and the expression of both qualities is encouraged. At the seventh chakra, the masculine and feminine unite and a person becomes a bi-gendered individual. The union of the inner masculine and feminine brings ecstasy.

Like the other chakras, the root chakra has three potentials. If the centre's energy is in balance then we will be calm, contented and connected to family and community. If the chakra's energy is moving downward, we will be stuck and unable to make important decisions, take action or move forward in life. We may become excessively attached to people, places or to objects. Excessive attachment cultivates greed, which may lead to the hoarding of wealth, power, or knowledge.

The upward movement of energy from the root chakra brings evolutionary changes and integration with higher chakras. We are no longer content with what we have been given by family, community, and culture. We become seekers and pilgrims, and begin the voyage to becoming true individuals. The true individual is someone who has been cleared of social and cultural programming. They are rooted in their own innate nature instead of in society and culture. They carry their home within.

Smell is of particular significance to the earth element and this chakra. Of the five senses, smell has the most direct connection to the brain and so our memory of smells is vivid, primal, and deep. Smell is the last sense to develop in a fetus and the first one to disappear when we die.

THE SECOND CENTRE: SEX OR ENERGY CHAKRA (SWADHISTHAN)

The Path of Energy

The second chakra is the centre of sex, which is often mistakenly equated with life energy. Although sex is just one of the many expressions of life energy, it is the most important as it is responsible for the survival of the species. This chakra is connected with the reproductive glands and the hormones of the testes, ovaries and uterus.

Of all the chakras, the second generates the most controversy because it is the centre for sex. Because sex is the most important expression of life, humans often want to control it in order to gain a sense of mastery over life. This is why the Sanskrit name for this chakra is *Swadhisthan*, which means "one who is the master of oneself."

The second chakra has three possible states. If the energy of the second chakra flows downward, then we become focused on sex, which leads to many mind and body problems. In this stuck state, time and energy are spent either in the contemplation of the sexual act or in the act itself. This eventually leads to corruption and decay as our energy stagnates. The first chakra, which brings rooting and a sense of belonging, is overtaken by sexual obsession. We may risk everything to indulge in sex.

The second state of the chakra is of balanced functioning, in which survival of the species is ensured, and pleasure is experienced through sexual union. Procreation is a universal human desire, and the birth of a child is celebrated in every culture. At a deep level, procreation is driven by the search for immortality—to see something of ourselves live beyond our own lifespan. The natural pleasure of sexuality has its own value apart from procreation, yet unfortunately sexuality is often distorted by rigid rules created by society, religion and culture. In many traditions, sex is only permitted for the purpose of procreation and not for pleasure. Due to these rules, there is often a sense of guilt and sin attached to sex. This repression of positive sexual energy can destroy the balanced functioning of the second chakra, with many negative consequences.

While balanced functioning of the second chakra is a source of inner pleasure and harmony, it is not enough to allow for evolution. When the energy of the second chakra moves upward, evolution to a higher state of being becomes possible. During the sexual act, seminal or vaginal fluid moves downward, carrying energy with it. When the second chakra's movement is upward, fluid will still flow downward but energy will move up toward the higher centres. The movement of this energy is felt as a stream of tingling sensation flowing inside the spine, bringing the experience of gentle orgasm. Later on this flow of energy becomes constant even without the sexual act and there is an ongoing feeling of bliss.

At this point, the excessive need for sex comes to an end and one may enter a natural state of celibacy. Celibacy here does not mean a withdrawal from sex, as it is a basic need and should be satisfied. In this context, celibacy means to satisfy the body's need for sex without excess.

At the highest levels of second chakra energy, sexuality becomes sacred. This is the ground on which Tantra is born. One of the Tantra's important messages is that sexuality can become a path to freedom. The word sacred doesn't mean that something is religious or spiritual. Sacred means that which can take us to a feeling of wholeness and well-being.

The sacredness of sex doesn't mean that it becomes a mechanical act devoid of pleasure. In sacred sex, bliss replaces pleasure, where pleasure is a momentary experience and bliss is constant. This bliss is born out of the awareness that we are not always our own masters. A master is not a controller but a witness and an observer. This awareness of self is the state of self-actualization or self-realization.

The element of the second chakra is water, which brings fluidity, movement, evolution and self-mastery. Evolution brings about the expansion of consciousness and knowledge and we develop greater psychological independence. That is the meaning of freedom or self-mastery. It is not physical independence but psychological freedom that the path of Naturality guides us towards.

THE THIRD CENTRE: SOLAR CHAKRA (MANIPURA)

Emotions; the Path of Passion and Action

Through the door of the third chakra, we enter the realm of feeling and emotion. At the third chakra, we become more conscious of ourselves and the world around us. We become aware of the multitude of connections that exist between events, and discover the complex wholeness that exists both within us and outside us.

When discussing the third chakra, it is important to study emotions, as they become increasingly more differentiated at the higher chakras. First, consider the difference between feeling and emotion. Emotions are the combination of many sensations, which are then expressed through meaningful behaviour. When emotions are felt consciously, they become feelings. Antonio Damasio describes this fact beautifully in his research. Similarly, there is an important distinction between perception and expression. In expression, the past and future play important roles, while in perception they do not. For example, thirst causes an emotion that arises out of the perception of various sensations present in the body. However, when we express that thirst by moving to quench it, we enter the realm of feeling. In the process of quenching our thirst, we must consider the past and future. We must evaluate factors such as the water's location, quality, quantity and availability.

Fear is the most fundamental emotion in all human beings, and it is present at all chakras. However, there is less conscious experience of it at the lower chakras, and so fear is not experienced as fully as at the higher centres. Some people refuse to grow, evolve and live fully because of the heightened fear they will experience at higher centres.

Since fear is present at all chakras, so are the mechanisms to escape that fear. While life continues in the forefront of our existence, fear is ever-present in the background. What we call "normal living" is a delicate balance we maintain in order to keep fear from dominating our daily lives. But we pay a price for escaping fear in this way. We only live a partial life, spending much of our time and energy creating devices to keep fear from emerging in our consciousness. Because of this, we are not fully in touch with ourselves.

The third centre is located around the navel area, connected to the solar plexus, and so is often called the solar chakra. This centre links to the enteric or "gut brain," which is part of the digestive system that includes the stomach, intestine, pancreas, spleen, and liver. Because of its connection to the rich nerve plexus and gut brain, the third chakra is very sensitive. When it doesn't function well, it can be the cause of many mind-body problems. This centre is the seat of emotion as well as action. The third chakra is also called the royal chakra, or the seat of the king and warrior, as it carries great power.

The element of the third chakra is fire and like the other chakras, this centre has three potentials. The first potential is of balance. When balanced, we are able to acquire power, wealth and glory through action in the world.

Downward movement from this chakra occurs when our fire energy doesn't find a means of expression. Downward movement dries the water element of the second chakra. Without the protection of water, fire energy rages out of control and burns us inside, emotionally and physically. We become filled with impotent anger and aggression and may destroy ourselves as well as those around us. In contrast, potent anger enables positive action and forward movement.

The third possibility at this chakra is the upward movement of energy. When the energy of fire moves up, old paths are cleared away and new ones are created. Most ordinary actions we carry out are actually reactions or reflexive actions that occur automatically without conscious awareness. Such reactions come from our cultural programming. However, when we become aware of our thoughts, words, and actions, we begin to live in a different way. Living with this awareness moves us out of the world of daily action and reaction, and leads us towards the unknown vastness of existence.

Vision is the sense connected with the energy of this centre. Clear eyes are needed to see the path, and passionate action is essential to move along it.

THE FOURTH CENTRE: HEART CHAKRA (ANAHAT)

Feelings, Dreams and Creativity; the Path of Love

The fourth chakra is the centre of feelings, particularly the feeling of love. Although emotions emerge at the third centre, they fully flower and are experienced in depth at the fourth. At the first centre, love is expressed as care, at the second as sex, at the third as passion, and at the fourth centre love is experienced as feeling.

Love is necessary to protect us from the fear that is ever-present in the back of our minds. In the absence of love, we succumb to fear and suffer from anxiety and panic, or we try to overcome it through aggression and violence. Both withdrawal from the world and lashing out at it occur due to an absence of love.

When love moves downward through the chakras, it becomes attachment and lust. When love moves upward, it is transformed into devotional love, in which we surrender to something higher than ourselves. Intense, passionate love towards someone else, in which there is a giving of oneself whole-heartedly to the other, is devotional love. This form of love contains within it a spark of the divine, and for many people, it is the beauty and intensity of human love that becomes the path to the sacred.

The fourth chakra is the centre of *Bhakti* or devotion, the seat of faith-based religious traditions. Most religious traditions are grounded in love and devotion to the Divine, and are based on faith rather than on intellectual analysis. Prayer is used to reach the Divine in these religious traditions.

The special sense of this centre is touch, and without touch, love remains unfulfilled. Whenever love emerges, there comes a deep longing to touch the object of that love. A sculptor wants to touch his work of art, a mother wants to touch her child, and a lover her beloved. There is a deep physiological link between the brain and skin, as both develop from similar embryonic tissue. The skin is an extension of the brain, for it is through the skin that the brain receives messages. Without touch, a person may not develop fully, psychologically or physically.

This chakra is also the centre of creativity, which is intimately connected with love. Love and creativity are inseparable companions. Love has always been a source of inspiration for painters, scientists, writers, and musicians. Without the love of something, it is not possible to be creative. During the process of creativity, energy moves up from the heart centre and connects with memories of touch, sounds, smells, feelings, and tastes in the brain, and links them to words, colors and images. This is how we form a piece of art, music, poetry, or a new scientific theory. When we become aware of the process of creativity, we feel this movement of energy.

Many creative people suffer because they remain at the fourth centre and feel fragmented within. Their daily lives don't reflect the incredible beauty they create in their work. The energetic experience of creativity and the existence of higher centres remain outside their awareness.

The fourth centre is the door to the personal subconscious and a step to universal unconscious. Conscious life is only the tip of the iceberg of our existence. We are conscious of only a small part of our totality, and the rest lies deep in our subconscious and unconscious. In the hidden dimensions of our being lie our motives, our conditioning, and all the unwritten history of our human heritage. This is where the primal past meets the present and affects the future. That hidden material and animal energy resides in a realm of light and darkness and is expressed through dreams. These dreams not only connect us to the animal and material world, but they also hold clues about our deeper identities. This realm contains our past, our creative energy, as well as our destiny.

Once we are able to connect with the energy of the subconscious and unconscious, we can begin to harness that energy and move to a state of wholeness. The barriers between the conscious, subconscious, and unconscious mind have to be demolished for this to occur. During such a process, a tremendous amount of energy is released in the brain, mind, and heart. By connecting with and harnessing that energy, a person becomes a shaman or a healer. A shaman is someone who has opened the door of the personal subconscious and walked courageously into the darkness of the universal unconscious, leaving behind all cultural conditioning.

At the fourth chakra, the primal sound of Om is heard spontaneously. The sound of Om or Amen vibrates in the depth of the universal subconscious. These sounds are present at the lower three chakras, but are in the form of undifferentiated vibrations. At the heart centre, this sound becomes audible. Primal sounds arise in solitude and without any contact with objects. In Sanskrit, it is called the *Anahat* sound—a sound that is produced without the striking of two objects or energies together. This is why the heart chakra is also called the Anahat chakra.

The fourth centre, with its primal energy, belongs to both the divine and the devil within us. Both divine and devil come from the same root word *Div*, which means "to shine." When the subconscious and unconscious energy of this centre is repressed or distorted, it takes the form of the devil. When the same energy finds its path and becomes conscious experience, it becomes the divine. Out of denial of one's true self, the "devil" is born, while full realization and acceptance of one's own unique being leads to the divine.

At this centre, the mythological worlds of gods and goddesses, demons and spirits emerge. While the origins of mythic thinking lie at the third centre, they come into full fruition at the fourth. It is at the fourth chakra that the mammalian brain intersects with the uniquely human component of the brain. This centre is the bridge between our material and animal past and our uniquely human present and divine future.

Wind, the element of the fourth chakra, gives one even more freedom to move and change. The water and fire elements have a greater capacity for movement than the earth element. The wind element moves faster than all three. This chakra is connected with the thymus gland, which is an important part of the immune system.

THE FIFTH CENTRE: THROAT CHAKRA (VISHUDDHA)

Science, Systems and Communication; the Path of Intellect

The fifth chakra is uniquely human. Complexity reaches its peak at this centre with the expression of logic, rationality, and language. Through these extraordinary faculties, human creativity is unleashed, and the universe of the mind is born. Here, science, systems of governance, and the idea of a universal moral order develop. Science becomes a powerful tool we can use to transform the outer world and control the forces of nature.

At the fifth centre, the rituals and traditions of the previous four chakras are left behind. Through logic, reason, and language, science emerges. Instead of praying to the ancestors of the first and second centres, and the gods and goddesses of the third and fourth, we start to take on the roles of those powerful spirits and gods.

At the fifth chakra, thoughts control the body and the environment. In this world created by the mind, we become gods. At this centre, thoughts are of supreme importance. Natural objects and phenomena are observed, labeled, and categorized; universal forces are discovered and uniform laws conceived; logical theories and systems are created, and science and technology make rapid progress.

The individual becomes the fundamental creative unit of the human world, rather than the family, group, or clan. Individual fulfillment takes priority over the fulfillment of the community.

The fifth chakra is the centre of discrimination, where, with the help of moral law and reason, we connect to society and work for the greater good. It is not the voice of gods or spirits, but written law that governs life. We are free to follow our own path as long as it doesn't conflict with social order and does not violate the rights of others.

When the throat chakra becomes active, there is an explosion of creativity. Creativity at the four lower centres is communal, limited, mythic and a part of daily living. Although creativity occurs at the fourth centre, it expresses itself fully at the fifth. The person becomes a creator.

When the fifth centre is in balance, the faculty of thinking, reasoning, and rationality function optimally. It enables us to make sound moral judgment and we do not succumb to superstition. Through analysis and synthesis, we arrive at rational conclusions that help us decide what actions to take. From this centre, *Jnana* or "knowledge" emerges. Jnana is central to Buddhism, Yoga and Vedantic Hinduism.

This centre also provides us with creative expression. We may be intensely creative within, but without the ability to express that creativity, we remain unfulfilled. Great teachers are creative, but also know how to communicate that creative energy. This is only possible if the fifth centre is open and functioning at its prime.

If we stay at the fifth centre, we may become trapped in the world of reason and rationality, products of the thinking mind. They are important milestones on the journey but are not the destination. However, the power of the mind is so great, and its creative expressions so complex, that it may seem as if the mind has mastered life. We may stay in the universe of the mind forever, never completing the journey towards wholeness. Mind can become a substitute universe.

The biggest problem at this chakra is that no experience remains pure, fresh and direct. All experiences are categorized into the "known" using memories, theories, concepts, definitions and beliefs. As the direct experiences of the lower four chakras move up, the force and energy of the fifth changes them forever. This centre thrives on predictability. We develop a strong aversion to the unknown or mysterious and thus we lose our sense of wonder.

If the energy of the fifth centre moves downward, we may succumb to illogical or irrational forces that hamper growth and wellness. This may give rise to extreme superstition and a cult mentality. Downward movement of the energy of this centre may also lead to the continuation of useless rituals and practices that are harmful, both physically and psychologically.

An upward movement of energy makes us more aware of the inner and outer world, which ultimately leads to wisdom. The Yoga of Knowledge is transformed into the Yoga of Wisdom. There is ample knowledge around us, but we need to discriminate what knowledge is relevant and beneficial for our inner development. The energy of the fifth chakra enables us to do this.

The element associated with the fifth chakra is space. It lies at the root of the neck and is connected to the cervical plexus, thyroid, and parathyroid glands. The vocal cords, also an instrument of expression, belong to this chakra. Sound is the special sense of this centre and is the first to appear at the fetus stage of development. It is also the last sense to disappear at death.

THE SIXTH CENTRE: THIRD EYE CHAKRA (AJNA)

Death and Naked Duality; the Path of Insight

The symbol representative of the sixth chakra is a lotus with only two white petals. This is in stark contrast to the complexity of the blue sixteen-petalled lotus, which is representative of the fifth centre. The complexity of the centre of reason and science gives way to the simplicity of the sixth centre. Here there are only two dimensions of existence, life and death.

At the sixth chakra, everything that supports us is left behind. The family and tribe of the first chakra, the pleasures of the second, the willful action of the third, the love of the fourth, and the reason and systems of the fifth chakra are all left behind and we are psychologically stripped. At the sixth centre, all existence is divided into two. In this state of clear duality of life and death, we stand alone before the universe as its object and adversary. The fear of death rises in the conscious mind, and there is no escape. Finally, life confronts death.

The fear of death becomes an unavoidable presence at this centre. In a dark and closed universe, we are left face to face with our own mortality. Life and death are always one, but the fear that arises out of self-awareness separates them. At the sixth centre, they face one other. This encounter is seen not through two ordinary eyes, but through the Third Eye of insight. Psychologically naked, we face a vast but enclosed universe where death is unavoidable. We are completely alone and surrounded by a universe hostile to us. The colour of this centre is white, which is the colour of peace, but also the colour of death.

A universe full of inescapable death is the universe of the existentialists. This dreadful universe seems to contain only angst and fear. Paradoxically, this brings us a kind of freedom. When we leave behind all supports and identities, we become free to make choices for which we are wholly responsible. Although there is a sense of total responsibility for our thoughts and actions, they seem pointless, even absurd, as everything seems to be moving towards death. It is a direct, uncensored experience of reality.

We are inconsolable because there is clear insight into the futility of all human efforts and the meaninglessness of existence. It is truly the opening of the third eye of Shiva, the god of dissolution. The opening of the third eye brings a painful and agonizing awareness of annihilation and death. When life and death come together in awareness, then there is an awakening. Normally one wants only to live, to escape from death. But in a life where there is psychological avoidance of death, living is incomplete and unfulfilled. Wholeness cannot be experienced if we do not face death.

Death brings an extraordinary state of total attention and focus. The brain becomes thoughtless yet fully aware of what is going on in the moment. All senses are alert and the noise of thoughts and emotions stop. It is a state of peace, where fear is replaced by tranquility.

At this chakra, our perception of reality is clear and we receive direct knowledge or insight. We are able to see from within. Until the fifth centre, our perception is conditioned. At the sixth chakra, all supports fall away, and the brain is relatively free to perceive reality directly. This activates certain abilities previously dormant in the brain. We may experience certain psychic powers. While thrilling, this can be detrimental to further progress if we become too attached to these unusual abilities.

Like all other centres, the energy of the sixth centre may move up or down. The downward movement of energy leaves one stuck in a state of anxiety and panic caused by a constant fear of death. Although there is deeper insight and intuition, we may be trying to constantly avoid situations that bring anxiety. This avoidance behavior can turn into the avoidance of life itself, as many situations that enrich life also tend to provoke anxiety. Life may begin to seem meaningless.

If the energy of the sixth centre moves upward, a new force pushes us towards true individuality and towards a sense of wholeness and wellness. With this upward movement of energy, life and death come together in full awareness, and we become masters of both mind and body. A teacher or guru is not necessary any more, as we are fully capable of moving forward alone on our inner journey. The Sanskrit name for this centre is *Ajna*, which means "command." This command of one's own self is not only psychological and existential, but it occurs at the physical level. It is a state of stillness and action. These two fundamental energies of life do not work in harmony before the sixth centre because there is a split between life and death. There is also inner conflict created by the clash between culture and our own nature.

The fully functional sixth centre brings peace to the heart and mind, as well as physical and physiological changes in the body. The body and mind move toward integration. A natural and spontaneous command over the body and mind is established. This is not the result of will or force—it is effortless. There arises a state of natural and effortless restraint that occurs without the interference of will. Such a state of restraint becomes part of life itself.

Another remarkable feature of this centre is the awareness of our dual nature in terms of gender. Our left brain is more masculine and is connected with 'I' or isolated personhood as well as with thoughts, language, details, analysis and action. It takes a pro-active or more aggressive approach to the world. The right brain is more feminine and is receptive, emotional, holistic, visual-spatial and imaginative and it is related to the feeling of "Amness." Amness is self-awareness in space, and is connected with art, music and abstract thoughts. In Indian tradition, this duality is depicted by Ardhanarishwar, a half-female, half-male image of Shiva and Parvati. The Yin-yang symbol also represents the same idea.

The pituitary gland is connected to the sixth chakra and plays a role in the regulation of all other endocrine glands.

THE SEVENTH CENTRE: CROWN CHAKRA (SAHASRARA)

Integration, Wholeness and Wellness; Arriving at the Peak of Evolution

At the seventh chakra there is a continuation of the experiences provided by the sixth centre. However, here we are reborn into wholeness, wellness, freedom and individuality. We discover our own centre, and we find our unique place in the world. Our mind-body begins to function as an integrated unit. We discover our individuality—not as an ideology, or as a renunciation or rejection of society. Rather, it is an integration of mind and body, which results in a peaceful transformation into a fully functional individual.

The seventh chakra is the final destination on our evolutionary journey. After this chakra, there is more to be discovered, but there is no path to walk or guide to follow. The seventh centre is not an independent chakra, but is born out of the integration and synthesis of the six previous chakras. The seventh chakra is the crown shrine, the pinnacle of personal achievement, and goes beyond anything represented by the other centres. No individual achievement can ever match the experience of living at this centre.

At the seventh chakra, a process of purification clears the clogged channels of communication in the mind and body, allowing energy to flow freely. There is an intimate communication between body and mind that binds cells with organs, organs with systems, and systems with one another. After this clearing, sensations connect with feelings, feelings with emotions, emotions with thoughts, thoughts with creativity, and creativity with wholesome living. In this state of complete interconnectedness, the body and mind function as an integrated unit. From this wholeness, the soul emerges. Although some people have glimpses of the soul or wholeness, very few are able to live in it, while still enjoying the fruits of the mind, body and the world.

The soul is a state of well-being. It contains the essence of all the lower chakras—the beauty of family, tribal or group ties, the pleasure of worldly things, passionate action, feeling and emotion, creativity and its expression and the ability to live fully in the presence of death. In this state of living, we know how to live simply and we understand what is essential and what is not. This simplicity contains all the complexities of life. We learn how to navigate these complexities but are never trapped by them. Simplicity is harmony in complexity.

The seventh chakra is the last piece of the mind-body puzzle. When it becomes fully functional and its energy moves upwards, the larger picture of our life becomes clear. The brain, the instrument of perception, is lit up from within and brain dormancy is over. Our wellness reserve becomes fully accessible. As the brain fills with delight and newfound energy, it becomes young again. The young brain is free from psychological conditioning and no longer dwells on the past or on dreams of the future. This brain is in communion with the moment. Such a brain is filled with passion and vibrates with the energy of wholeness. It doesn't require any external stimulation to experience an ongoing state of passion.

The physical body goes through the natural process of aging, but a brain that vibrates with the energy of wholeness remains fresh and passionate even at the time of death. A brain that is dependent on external stimuli for its passion and energy will wither as soon as that external support is gone. Withdrawal from external supports happens naturally as we age. In old age, we become less involved with family and community and the body's capacity for sensual pleasure diminishes. But a brain fuelled by its own inner resources and energy is its own master and continues to be aware, passionate and full of delight. This is a state of freedom and integration, individuality and independence.

We are often confused about what independence truly means. We think that independence is the capacity to make certain decisions on our own, to live separately or to create our lives through the choices we make. This is a type of freedom—however, we are still dependent on the world for pleasure. If the outer world is in chaos, then our inner world is shaken as well. But an awakened brain is not dependent on the external world for joy. A person with an awakened brain is sometimes referred to as a Fakir or a "kingly beggar"—someone who needs a basic minimum to survive, but beyond that, is not dependent on the world. This individual can choose a life of complete simplicity because the brain is no longer victim to habit and addiction.

AWAKENING OF THE ENERGY CENTRES

After awakening of the chakras, we may perceive sensations not only in the body but also at the locations of the chakras. Sometimes, the energy of an awakened chakra may be particularly intense and may produce mild discomfort or at times pain. We may either feel intense sensation or a feeling of whirling energy. The pain we may feel after the chakras awaken is the result of a surge of energy rising through the body, clearing the channels as it moves. This pain may be particularly intense in the chest and head, and may be mistaken for a heart attack.

The energy of the first chakra is usually felt either in the perineum or at the lower end of the spine. The energy of the second chakra is usually felt in or just above the genital area or at a corresponding point on the back. The third chakra's energy is felt in front of the body between the belly button and the pit of the stomach or at the back. The energy of the fourth chakra is felt in the front of the chest and the fifth's is felt at the root or back of the neck. The energy of the sixth centre is usually experienced on the forehead, and the energy of the seventh is felt on top of or all over the head.

We may also experience a unique feeling on the back of the neck, chest and abdomen. When the chakras become active and both the moon and sun channels are functioning at their peak, energy finds its way into the central channel. At this point, it flows like a stream, starting at the lower end of the spine, moving up towards the brain. As the stream of sensation reaches the brain, it takes the form of a rising spring, flowing to the top of the brain and then falling back to soak the whole brain with sensation. This is called the Fountain Effect.

When the cells, organs, nerves, spinal cord and brain are flooded with energy, purification of the body and brain occurs. All the accumulated emotional memories that affect that way we think and behave are washed away. Although the conditioned mind is washed away in the process of awakening, our technical intelligence (essential for survival), innovative thinking and emotional expression remain intact. Once the brain is freed from its past conditioning, a new energy that heals and brings wellness is released. The emotional grip of memory is released and we no longer react to it. At this point, we are no longer victims of the trauma, tragedies, abuse, anger, hatred, grief and guilt of the past. The body and the brain function with their own natural rhythm.

This movement of energy may produce a hot or tingling sensation in the spinal cord, while in the brain, it may create pressure or the sound of thunder. Often one experiences ecstasy, although this can turn into pressure and headaches if the process intensifies.

EXPERIENCE OF EXPANSIVENESS

Chakras can also be thought of as windows to the universe. As each chakra allows a particular part of the brain and body to become fully functional, a window to a new world opens. The activation of the chakras is not only about integration at an individual level but about reintegration with the larger universe. The microcosm of the body and brain doesn't function in isolation from the macrocosm. However, when the brain and body are not fully functional, we are seldom aware of that connection. Without an intimate relationship with nature and the earth, we are unable to treat them with compassion. Whatever relationship we have with nature tends to be intellectual or emotional, but devoid of any deep connection. We are thus able to destroy it without remorse. Once the chakras are open, however, we experience a profound intimacy with the earth. We see ourselves in the context of larger natural forces. The human-made world is not rejected. Instead, it becomes an extension of the natural world. In this way, we finally find our home within both the natural and human-made world. When one's home lies within, there is never a feeling of alienation. This is the experience of expansiveness.

At the seventh chakra, we do not become completely free from grief, anger, sensuality, hatred or violence. Rather, in witnessing awareness, the brain becomes like the waxed petal of a lotus flower. Events, reactions and emotions touch the brain but quickly fall away without leaving a mark. This is the beginning of a state called *Turiya*. Turiya simply means "the fourth state" and is an experience of tranquility, like that of a deep sleep, but with full awareness.

At the seventh chakra there is no gender. Until the sixth, one is either male or female but at the seventh, the inner feminine and masculine meet and embrace each other, resulting in an asexual union. Pleasure is experienced during this union, although it is no longer a sexual union. True celibacy emerges at this point because the need for the external male or female diminishes. Various spiritual traditions around the world depict this union using a half male, half female deity.

The darkness of death, which brings tremendous fear at the sixth chakra, is resolved at the seventh. Death is an ever-present reality and is accepted as a part of living. However, it should be noted that the body still responds to danger with fear, and we remain concerned about our well-being. In fact, we worship life more than ever. Living is full of delight, and so to waste it or to end it carelessly becomes even more undesirable. The basic biological fear of death stays, as it is a natural protective response. However, our psychological fear of death comes to an end.

At the seventh chakra, we arrive at the boundaries of time and space. For the first time, we feel that these boundaries are not ultimate truths and that there is more to discover beyond them. This is the result of a shift in our consciousness. Just for a moment, our consciousness moves from the edge of the crown chakra into a realm that is beyond the individual. This momentary movement gives us a glimpse of universal consciousness.

FULL FUNCTIONING OF THE BRAIN

When the chakras are awakened, there is a free flow of energy that connects them. The effect of such an awakening on the dormant brain and body is remarkable. They begin to produce their own pleasure chemicals, creating a state of inner joy. This results in the emergence of a natural austerity. We eat, sleep, work, exercise and are involved in sexual activity only as much as is needed to maintain the health of the brain and body. This is not a forced austerity—rather, body and mind function at their optimal efficiency naturally. Although this lifestyle may seem frugal, it is actually a rich and natural way of living. The senses are sharp and the brain is exquisitely sensitive, needing very little outer stimulation. We live with effortless passion.

When the brain is awakened, we become true individuals. It is the ultimate flowering of our potential. On the journey from the first chakra to the seventh, we undergo the process of individuation. The many forms of conditioning are gradually put aside, and the fragmented mind slowly comes into harmony with itself.

Opposing forces come to be seen as one truth and part of one movement. The individual achieves an undivided perspective, where all things move in dynamic balance and wholeness. This wholeness is neither perfect nor symmetrical but rather it is *natural*. We feel a sense of natural harmony within. Although our external life may be filled with complexity and chaos, we are able to function with ease and grace. In this state there is not only an awakening of the brain but of each cell, organ and system in the body. Sensations are felt as a stream of vibrations flowing from the periphery of the body towards the centre and from the lower parts of the body to the upper parts. Nerve impulses move from peripheral nerves towards the spinal cord and brain. This is felt throughout the day and night, without interruption. To the individual, it feels as though the body is vibrating and there is a sense of gentle pleasure.

REGRESSION AND PROGRESSION

In times of crisis, a person may either progress to a higher chakra or regress to a lower chakra. A crisis which brings the progression or regression of this kind includes war, natural disasters, or personal trauma and tragedy. A mature ego is formed by the five chakras of the body, emotions, feelings and intellect. Ego's consciousness is conditioned, but it gives a person stability to face the turmoil and chaos of life. In regression, the ego slides down to the lower chakras of emotions or the chakras of the body. This regression can psychologically paralyze the person, or it can result in a dangerous loss of individuality in which the person simply surrenders to the ideas of others (mob mentality).

Times of crisis can also cause progression to a higher chakra. The crisis can challenge a person to search more avidly for answers, and thus move up to a higher chakra—perhaps from the emotion-focused outlook of the fourth chakra to the more reasoned perspective of the fifth chakra. Some people may even go through the existential crisis of the sixth chakra and arrive at the seventh. This brings about the transformation to a fully functional individual.

INVOLUTION: "CURLING IN ON ITSELF"

Involution occurs when the conscious energy of a chakra starts folding in on itself. At the end of evolution at the seventh chakra, the inner lamp of one's consciousness is lit. With this newfound state of awareness, we begin to descend from the seventh chakra through the sixth and all the way down to the first. This descent is radically different than what was experienced during the initial ascent from the first to the seventh. In ascent and evolution, we leave behind social and cultural centres and discover our own natural centre. In descent and involution, we transcend even that centre and go beyond individuality. It is the experience of universal consciousness both within and without. There is now only one consciousness, and it begins to fold in on itself. Consciousness starts to become conscious of itself.

We can visualize the processes of evolution and involution as a fountain. A water stream bursts upward from the earth (evolution) and at the crown centre it becomes a fountain. It then falls like an umbrella to the earth, covering a much wider area (involution). We can also call this the Banyan Phenomenon. The banyan tree has long branches that reach upward, then fall like an umbrella, covering a wide area of earth around the tree.

Evolution reaches its peak at the seventh chakra when we become individuals. The mind and body function as one unit. Our consciousness is not external, social or cultural but is established in our own mind-body complex. We feel anchored within. Our social and cultural roles may continue but they lose their previous significance.

Our true identity is rooted in our own mind-body nature or innate nature. There is a clear awareness of the world outside and of the world within. Even when lost in inner and outer turmoil, we recover quickly. Self-esteem comes from within, so it is sustained despite successes or failures.

However, even at the seventh chakra our perception is still dual, where experience and experienced remain different. But as we move into the process of involution, something radically different happens. We transcend any kind of centre, whether it is a cultural, societal or innate. It is a centre-less state and we are released into universal consciousness which is everywhere and in all things, both living and non-living. This is an experience of oneness.

Involution to the Sixth Chakra

The sixth chakra is the chakra of existential despair and fear. Involution to the sixth chakra brings the experience of universal despair, which is hidden in the heart of all human beings. This gives us insight into universal fear and suffering. It is not an intellectual or emotional comprehension—rather, it is experienced directly through the eyes of wisdom and compassion. However, the fear, despair and suffering we experience here leave no lasting mark on us.

Involution to the Fifth Chakra

The fifth chakra is the chakra of intellect and logic. Involution to the fifth chakra brings the experience of wisdom. The intellect and logic of the fifth turns into universal wisdom and insight. Wisdom at this level means that we gain an understanding of the state of humanity by knowing why human beings are in fear, conflict and discontent. We understand the solution that is needed to free them from this state. An ability to articulate and present solutions to problems faced by humanity also develops at this level. *Jnana* or knowledge becomes *Jnana Yoga* or Yoga of knowledge.

Involution to the Fourth Chakra

The fourth chakra is the chakra of feeling. Involution to the fourth chakra transforms the feeling of love into universal love and compassion. Love and devotion becomes *Bhakti Yoga*.

Involution to the Third Chakra

The third chakra is the chakra of emotion, will and passion. Involution to the third chakra brings the experience of universal will, passion and action. Ordinary action becomes *Karma Yoga*.

Involution to the Second Chakra

The second chakra is the chakra of life, energy and sex. Involution to the second chakra brings the experience of universal energy or *Shakti*.

Involution to the First Chakra

The first chakra is the chakra of matter and death. Involution to the first chakra is the most difficult. Here we experience universal matter as a biologically alive and conscious entity. Matter is the densest component of existence and the most difficult to penetrate because consciousness is hidden deep within it. At this chakra there is no difference between life and death. They become one, because at the level of matter and biology death and life are still not separated.

HISTORY AND THE CHAKRAS

"Humans don't create history. History creates human beings."

We have seen that the concepts of Kundalini and the chakras can be used as a powerful metaphor for understanding the expression of consciousness. We can also use the chakras as a way of understanding human history and imagining the future of humanity.

As we observed earlier, the fear of death and life starts at the first chakra. As evolution moves forward, the expression of consciousness increases and with it comes more knowledge of life and death. More knowledge of life becomes the source of enjoyment but more knowledge of death creates more fear and anxiety. A framework for understanding these fundamental facts of life is needed. At the second, third and fourth chakras, people coped by worshipping and praying to the elements of nature, gods, goddesses and spirits and finally God.

But at the fifth chakra something changed. With the discovery of new tools of reason and science, humans started to take control of the material world. An explosion of creativity and technology gradually transformed the way people related to the world. Technology brought unprecedented comfort and pleasure. For increasing numbers of people, God was replaced by science and technology.

However, fear and anxiety about death did not go away. Instead of turning to the old gods, spirits and God, humans created an increasing complex material world. In this world, more and more safeguards against danger were established in order to create an illusion of immortality. Along with this, humans increasingly focused on material consumption, living in the world with as much pleasure as possible.

As we are increasingly aware, the rapid spread of this consumer culture around the world is depleting the world's resources at an alarming rate. Although it is clear that this is an unsustainable way of living, nobody seems ready to listen and change their lives. A consumer is an addict and the consumption is an addiction. Except for a very few, most of us are involved in this consumer culture, a massive movement which cuts across race, religion and countries.

As we continue to deplete the earth's resources, we are moving towards an inevitable environmental disaster. From a human point of view, it seems that these environmental disasters and their impact on life on earth is a catastrophe created by the bad choices made by humans. We have the will and freedom to make better choices for our own future and for the rest of the planet. But even if that change begins to happen, we have already come too far along this destructive path. Environmental disasters loom ahead of us, creating a grim picture of the future of humanity.

But can we think about this scenario from a different perspective? Suppose we once again turn to the chakras as a metaphor for the expression of human consciousness. If environmental disaster occurs, this profound crisis may have the effect of bringing a radical change in the consciousness of a significant number of people. They will be pushed into the chaos of the sixth chakra, where life and death face each other in stark opposition. But this is not the end; when they move through this stage into the light of the seventh chakra, an awakening of individual consciousness will happen. That will be the beginning of an entirely new era.

So, from this perspective, environmental disaster will be a force that will push us to the next stage of evolution. All evolutionary leaps come with catastrophe. Whether it is an individual or the whole humanity, without the shattering of the old, the radically new can't happen.

Up to fifth chakra, the unfolding of history is not a conscious process in humans. We become aware of history when it has already unfolded; we cannot influence or control the process. Only a person who becomes conscious of the subconscious forces that are forming history can participate as a mindful observer or witness.

Beyond the sixth chakra, people will begin to experience the true intimations of sacred wholeness and well-being. At the seventh chakra, witnessing consciousness will arise. We will realize that humanity's future is divine and evolution won't stop until we experience the non-dual oneness of the cosmos. So, in spite of darkness and disasters, there is no place for pessimism. How could there be pessimism if the whole cosmos is the expression of timeless and eternal consciousness? But in order to arrive there we must be prepared to endure the shocks and trauma of the forward thrust of evolution.

Chapter 5

THE SCIENCE OF NATURALITY

In the previous two chapters, we have been exploring the concept of Naturality psychologically and philosophically. We used Ayurvedic understandings of the body and mind to explore Prakirti —our innate nature. Then we explored the concept of Kundalini and the chakras as a way of understanding life energy.

But can we examine the concepts of Naturality using a modern, scientific lens? All Naturality has an underpinning of human biology. If ancient and modern "ways of knowing" can lead to greater understanding of Naturality, then the relevance of these teachings will truly shine forth. In the following section, we will connect Naturality with some fundamental features of brain anatomy and physiology. This connection will describe the path of Naturality as a way of being that reflects both ancient and modern understandings of human evolution and evolution.

EVOLUTION OF THE HUMAN BRAIN

Universal Nature is the source of all that exists. Universal Nature is primal, without a beginning or an end, and from that boundless and infinite energy the universe comes into being. From the most primitive life forms, a process of evolution towards greater and greater complexity began. It took billions of years for the human brain to evolve into its present form, the most marvellous instrument of perception in the universe.

Through the brain and the sense organs, we consciously experience the world. The brain and the body are intimately linked, acting upon each other in a seamless fashion. Together, the brain and body make it possible for us to survive in the world, to interact with other living beings, and to experience a range of emotion.

Because our brain was fashioned by Nature, the brain is capable of revealing Nature's secrets and intelligence. This is why it is sometimes referred to as the "three-pound universe." If consciousness can tune into the brain in a certain way, the structure, function and underlying interconnectedness of the cosmos, both materially and spiritually ,will be revealed. It will also reveal the underlying interdependence and oneness of life and consciousness, which is the experience of liberation.

Each one of us has an innate nature that is unique, and yet is part of the universal Nature. As we become more conscious of our own inner nature, we begin to get glimpses of the universal Nature. We discover that individual and universal Nature is one and the same. We realize that the microcosm contains the macrocosm and macrocosm contains the microcosm. In other words, the drop contains the sea and the sea contains the drop.

THE EXPRESSION OF CONSCIOUSNESS

Primal consciousness is infinite and contains all possible forms of consciousness, which can be experienced by living beings. What is experienced depends on how developed the brain is. At a particular level of brain development, a new form of consciousness is experienced. Mirroring and perception begin with unicellular organisms. Before this, consciousness lies buried deep within matter.

As our brain develops and vibrates at a particular frequency, we experience a specific level of consciousness. As self-aware human beings, we can change the structure and physiology of our brain and become conscious of those experiences that are not available to other living beings. This is conscious evolution. Within us, all possible levels of consciousness are already there, so consciousness itself does not evolve. Rather, the brain evolves and gains more and more access to it.

All creative and spiritual practices are about changing the structure and physiology of the brain in order to tune into more conscious experience. We have the potential to become conscious of every evolutionary frequency of the brain, eventually arriving at a point where the frequency becomes almost infinite or zero. Here we tune into a primal consciousness. This gives us the experience of non-duality, Nirvana or the feeling of timeless and spaceless existence.

In this process of evolution there are no unpredictable leaps. What we consider a "leap" is the result of a slow build-up of evolutionary movement that reaches a critical threshold. This is when a new state of consciousness is perceived. Also, there are no sharp boundaries between evolutionary stages—they overlap and merge with one another. Evolutionary movement is like the formation of a river. The river begins its journey drop by drop from a melting glacier in the mountains. These drops become a trickle, and this trickle a stream and this stream turns into a river. As the river flows down the valley, it becomes wide and powerful and eventually merges with the sea. Water from the sea evaporates into the sky and falls in the mountains, returning to its original source. This cycle repeats and continues. All these stages overlap and there are no clear divisions between each stage.

In advanced animals, the brain is responsible for emotions. In humans it has brought the wonders of self-awareness, through which we are able to experience feelings and emotions as well as reflect on the past and contemplate the future. We are capable of logical thinking, which has unleashed endless creativity and has led to the emergence of science, art, ethics, religion and culture. But above all of this is the incredible ability we possess to feel the presence of the infinite and eternal, the source of the universe itself. The infinite is not an empty void but contains all that is possible, was possible and will be possible. People have given this feeling of boundless and timeless existence many names including God, Brahman and so on.

PHYSICAL CONSCIOUSNESS: THE PRIMAL BRAIN

Unicellular and multi-cellular organisms.

The evolution of the brain can be visualized as an image of the Tree of Life. Different stages of evolution correspond with the various parts of the tree, beginning with inert matter and energy in which consciousness is hidden, although present. The first active expression of consciousness is in the form of a single cell, which represents the consciousness of the body in its most rudimentary form. The entire cell functions as a brain because nothing is differentiated. However, this single cell is the seed of the fully differentiated human body and brain.

Early physical consciousness is reflexive, without the capacity for self-awareness or reflection. Sensation is the mode of perception that helps in attraction and repulsion towards the positive and negative environment. Primal fear appears at this stage of consciousness as repulsion, which helps in moving away from dangers in the environment. Survival and reproduction, which occur in a repetitive and fixed pattern, are the only mode of living and are completely controlled by nature. There is inner silence without any language, but that silence is brimming with life's energy. The body is in communion with the material universe without any sense of time and space.

This level is the ground upon which the tree of life grows. If we become conscious of this level of existence, then it leads to non-dual materialism in which matter becomes conscious of itself and is in communion with the rest of the material universe.

PHYSICAL CONSCIOUSNESS: THE REPTILIAN BRAIN

In the ground of the cell and body, the roots and stems of the tree of life evolve and grow. Nerve roots, the spinal cord and the brain stem form. The brain stem is the reptilian brain where consciousness emerges but without the element of self-awareness or self-reflection. The brain stem has centres for the circulatory and respiratory systems, and communicates with the body through the spinal cord and nerve roots. This helps in the maintenance of homeostasis or dynamic balance.

At this level, the organism lives in survival and reproduction mode with all systems controlled by nature in a predictable pattern. Perception occurs through a complex combination of sensations. There are sounds but no language and no mental boundaries or attachments. There is no sense of time and space. The world of names and forms has not been born. The organism lives in an unconscious eternity.

It is possible to become aware of this level of existence and this experience is called Non-Duality or Void or Nothingness. This consciousness at its primitive level can be stimulated by jogging, climbing, running, exercising, dancing, extreme sports, physical yoga and the sweat lodge experience.

In summary, the body with physical consciousness at the reptilian brain level is the root and stem of the tree of life.

EMOTIONAL CONSCIOUSNESS: THE MAMMALIAN BRAIN

Emotional consciousness occurs in the limbic system or mammalian brain. This is where the pleasure centers and the centres for the autonomic nervous system, vital for homeostasis and mind-body interface, are located. At the level of the mammalian brain, the non-dual state of the body and the reptilian brain are split into the duality of subject and object. This duality is perceived moment to moment rather than in a linear fashion. Self-awareness arises for the first time, but only briefly. Experience is based on emotions, not reason. Nature still plays the primary role in the organism's development but nurture starts contributing in a significant way to growth.

Consciousness becomes somewhat reflective and attachment becomes part of living. Mental boundaries are drawn, creativity is expressed, life and death are separated and existence is purposeful. The world of time-space and name-form is born. It is possible to become aware of emotional consciousness, which leads to living moment-to-moment.

Emotional consciousness forms the branches and leaves of the tree of life. This level of consciousness can be stimulated through music, chanting, singing, sex, breathing, yoga, extreme sports, trauma and emotional arousal ("emotional trance").

INTELLECTUAL CONSCIOUSNESS: THE HUMAN BRAIN

With the development of the neo-cortex and prefrontal cortex in humans, the size and weight of the brain increase. At this stage of evolution, humans develop logic, rationality, language and the ability to plan for the future. Through these extraordinary faculties, human creativity is unleashed, and the universe of the mind is born. Science, systems of governance, and the idea of a universal moral order grow out of this universe.

Thoughts are of supreme significance. Natural objects and phenomena are observed, labeled, and categorized; universal forces are discovered and uniform laws conceived; logical theories and systems are created, and science and technology make rapid progress. The individual becomes the fundamental creative unit of the human world. Accordingly, individual fulfillment takes precedence over the fulfillment of the community. The formation of self or ego is complete. We have now developed the ability to reflect about our thoughts and actions.

At this level of development, raw and direct experiences that emerge from the reptilian and mammalian brain are changed and categorized before they reach our consciousness. Everything goes through a process of conditioning. All experiences are filtered and changed by the old and known. Nothing "new" is experienced.

Although the three components of the brain are not separate, socio-cultural conditioning of the neo-cortex dominates one's life. We essentially become social animals rather than fully functional individuals with unique innate natures. This results in a persistent sense of frustration and a loss of well-being. This cycle may continue for a long time unless trauma, suffering, a sensitive nature, disillusionment or a search for meaning pushes us into the next stage of evolution.

Intellectual consciousness forms the flowers and fruits of the tree of life.

RIGHT AND LEFT BRAIN

The Western concept of the Ego or self differs from the Eastern. In the West, the Ego or self is primarily a sense of "I" while in the East it is the feeling of "I Am." "I" is achieved when intellectual consciousness is added to emotional and physical consciousness but they don't function in unison and harmony. "I Am" contains all three types of consciousness working in harmony, which results in mind-body integration. "I" belongs to the left brain and is primarily connected with linear time. "Amness" is related to the right brain, which is being aware of one's existence in the here and now. "I" has sense of time while "Amness" has a sense of space.

Many functions of the left and right brain overlap. However, in certain areas of functioning, they have distinct roles. The right brain is intuitive and has a circular or network memory, which doesn't have the sequential quality of the left brain. This side of the brain is more peaceful, creative, artistic, imaginative and aesthetic. Closely connected to the limbic system, this side of the brain is linked to emotional states and is more interconnected and interdependent than the left brain. The right side of the brain also appears to play a role in mystical experiences, as well as in the experiences of sex and love. Yoga, meditation, music, arts, and extreme sports can help us tap into this brain.

RIGHT BRAIN MEMORY

When sequential memory (located in the left brain) is damaged, the right brain can compensate. Although the left brain will always play a role, the right brain compensates by creating a memory mechanism that is mainly impressionistic, emotional and experience-based. Right-brain memory is like *Indra's net of jewels* (a metaphor for the interconnectedness and interdependence of all life), in which each point of memory is like a switch that, if pressed, will light up the whole network of memory. Each point reflects the whole. We can call this type of memory "linking memory" or "image memory."

Such memory is used in Indian classical music. A musician can play a raga, which may last up to three hours, entirely from memory without written music. Using this type of memory stimulates spontaneous creativity because we are accessing the limbic, creative brain through the right brain.

LEFT BRAIN

The left brain is a newer development and doesn't have a counterpart within the older parts of the brain. The left brain is innovative but not creative, in that it can improve and perfect existing creative expression, but raw creativity always emerges from the limbic system or emotional brain. The particular characteristics of the left brain include a sense of time and connection to past, present and future (a sense of "I" ness). The functions of the left brain are more analytical than the right brain, with cognitive capacities of reason and logic. Memory is linear and sequential. Thoughts are structured, bounded and confined by limits.

EXISTENTIAL CONSCIOUSNESS: THE EXPERIENCE OF DISINTEGRATION

At this stage, the tree of life is shaken. Here, the prefrontal and neo-cortex lose their dominance and the turbulent energy of the mammalian and reptilian components of the brain take over. This results in mental chaos and loss of cognitive control and a sense of self and identity. In existential consciousness, social and cultural customs, rewards and achievements are stripped of their meaning and we are left psychologically naked and exposed. We become fully conscious of our fear of death and life.

Everything that has supported us, both externally and internally, is left behind. The family and tribe, the pleasures of life and action are all abandoned. The mythic worlds of God, gods, and spirits as well as the realm of logic, reason, and science no longer accompany us. All of existence is divided in two, a clear duality, in which the person—as the subject—stands in front of the universe as its object and adversary. Finally life confronts death.

NEUROPLASTICITY

Neuroplasticity is the innate ability of the brain to change itself with new experiences. It used to be thought that brain cells could not change or regenerate, and that once damage was done it was irreversible. However, we now know that the human brain has a remarkable ability to change and reorganize itself by forming new neural connections. Research done on long-time meditators such as Buddhist monks has shown that the brain is flexible and can be changed even to the last moment of life.

When we read the writings of the sages, we realize that the concept of brain malleability is not new. Their concept was that both the body and brain could be changed and transformed by inner and outer experiences. That change can be positive (positive neuroplasticity) when we can erase negative patterns of traumatic experiences, or it can be negative (negative neuroplasticity) such as in case of chronic pain when the pain is projected on the body from the brain.

On the path of Naturality, neuroplasticity is of great significance. As we learn to live according to our nature, our brain become more and more free from past conditioning and eventually the brain is changed radically in the experience of liberation. It begins to function as a harmonious and integrated unit, filled with awareness, bliss and compassion (the ABC of life).

Sri Aurobindo and his spiritual companion, the Mother of Pondicherry, went even further, experiencing and describing a radical transformation of the body at the cellular level. Similar experiences were reported by the contemporary sage U. G. Krishnamurti. We can call this Somato-plasticity (the word *Soma* in Greek means "body"). But as yet, there is no scientific explanation for this phenomenon—it will take time before scientists can discover this secret of the body.

WITNESSING CONSCIOUSNESS: INTEGRATION AND WHOLENESS

The chaos and disorganization of the existential crisis is like the pupa stage of a butterfly's life cycle. After the smooth development of the larva, the pupa loses all symmetry and organization and becomes like featureless glue. Even the genetic material breaks down, becoming scattered and without pattern. But out of this chaos, a butterfly emerges ready to fly.

In the state of integration and wholeness we become fully functional individuals with natural and spontaneous witnessing consciousness. One of the early signs of this state is a sense of well-being which becomes an ever-present feeling. At this stage the tree of life achieves full growth. The characteristics of witnessing consciousness are as follows:

- The reptilian, mammalian and neo-cortex complexes work in harmony. This is experienced as "flow," or bliss.
- The brain functions as one and as an integral part of the body. This is experienced as oneness of mind and body.
- The brain is awakened and dormancy is over. This leads to the activation of pleasure centers, bringing a sense of well-being.
- Increased connectivity and communication exist between various parts of the brain and the body. This results in a feeling of wholeness. This is also felt in the form of tingling sensations in the body and a fountain of energy intermittently pouring into the brain.
- The prefrontal cortex thickens and more mirroring properties of neurons are activated, resulting in witnessing consciousness.

The integration of the neo-cortex, limbic system and reptilian complex allows our innate nature to express itself in physical, emotional and intellectual intelligence. The expression of innate nature is the realization of our genetic potential and the epigenetic influences with which we are born. Although our acquired conditioning (post birth) is gone, our conditioning from our past life, parent's genes and the influences of ancestors are still with us.

The integration of the various components of the brain produces a sustained release of energy. This energy rushes through the brain and body and washes away the memories of past traumas and suffering. Healing occurs. This sustained energy flow is experienced as passion and persistent pleasure. Also, the release of energy from the mammalian and reptilian parts of the brain helps us to connect our experiences in various ways, which can result in an outpouring of creativity.

Destiny, hidden in our genetic and epigenetic heritage, is discovered with the awakening of innate nature. We realize what our unique contribution can be—what we were born to do. As we develop this witnessing consciousness, we are able to accept mortality as a part of life. Time moves from moment to moment and we experience spontaneous meditation.

Chapter 6

THE SEVEN DOORS TO NATURALITY

So far, we have been exploring what the path of Naturality means, and how walking this path can lead us to an understanding of our own innate nature. Now we will turn to some practical tools that can assist us in walking that path. We call these tools "the seven doors to Naturality". Each of these doors can reveal a way to progress towards a state of freedom from fear. But it's important to note that none of these "seven doors to Naturality" represents a fixed and rigid regimen that dictates exactly what one must or mustn't do. Rather, these doors offer us opportunities and ideas - but we must fill in the details ourselves. The seven doors take into consideration our innate nature, or Prakirti, with which each one of us is born. We must find out what resonates best with *our* mind and body. We can open and enter more than one door to Naturality. Our Naturality efforts can integrate all seven or some of those seven doors because they are not contradictory but complimentary to each other.

There is no Guru on the path of Naturality. Instead, there are teachers of Naturality, who can play a role at the very beginning of the inner journey. They may point out something or explain certain ideas and experiences. Once we are firmly established on the path to Naturality, there is no longer a need for guidance. It is a self-directed journey.

THE SEVEN DOORS TO NATURALITY

1. Natural Ethics: Self-care and care for others
2. Self-Knowing: Studying the book of life
3. Worship and Prayer
4. Fasting and Pilgrimage
5. Yoga Poses and Movements
6. Breathing Exercises
7. Meditation

NATURAL ETHICS: SELF-CARE AND CARE FOR OTHERS

"We cannot play life's symphony without practicing the notes of ethics."

Dharma means "the natural laws which sustain the inner and outer universe." Ethics should be in accordance with Dharma because living according to Dharma is a natural way of living. To understand ethics is to discover the inherent laws and principles of living. When we live in an ethical way, we integrate the traditions and customs of a specific society and culture and live harmoniously in that environment.

Naturality can't grow and flower without ethics. An ethical boundary is not a prison but a fence that protects the individual and the community at large. Such protection brings the sense of trust and ease needed for the process of Naturality to unfold.

The first principle of ethics is self-care. We must take care of our body, our feelings and emotions, as well as our intellect and soul.

Without proper self-care, we can't take care of others. If we are healthy and happy, only then we can make others healthy and happy. Through self-care we experience emotional and cognitive intelligence. In turn, this leads to the experience of soul or wholeness.

On the path of Naturality, ethics are not detailed instructions on how to think, behave or live. It's not a rigid set of rules to govern and manage life. It is about discovering the innate ethical sense that is embedded in our biology, brain and body. Natural ethics must go hand in hand with the social and cultural environment of our time and place. While social and cultural ethics are more or less the same for any given community or group, natural ethics differ from person to person because they are connected to our unique innate nature. For example, compassion is to be expressed differently from person to person. In an Earth person, compassion is expressed through the direct care of others, while in a Fire person it is expressed through meaningful leadership. Wind people express compassion through creative thought and action that helps to alleviate suffering. Within this framework, we each have our own way of thinking and behaving ethically.

The following mantra is the mantra of Naturality ethics:

> Dharma Daham, Dharma Manas,
> Dharma Buddhi-Atman
>
> ***Right care to body, feelings, mind and soul***
>
> Dharma Priya Jan, Dharma Serva Jan,
> Dharma Desh, Dharma Dhara
>
> ***Right care to family, commu-***
> ***nity, country and the earth***
>
> Dharma Neham, Dharma Ekam,
> Dharma Hee Gatisheelta

Let feeling of love and oneness sustain right care

Dharma Jeevan, Dharma Chetan,
Dharma Hee Ananda Param

Let right care bring the bliss
of conscious existence

Self-care has seven components that contribute to wellness. They are governed by the innate nature of the body and mind, and discovered through the study of one's own life. These seven components are: sleep; food; exercise; relationships; work; home life and mind-body practice.

SEVEN SELF-CARE STEPS TOWARDS NATURALITY

To be on the path of Naturality gives us the extra responsibility of taking care of our body and mind. We need to eat nutritious food, of good quality and appropriate quantity. We must ensure that we have enough rest and sleep, that we exercise the body and live in harmonious relationships with others. The home where we live should be clean and should suit our innate nature or Prakirti. We should practice those asanas, pranayams and meditation practices that are suited for our mind and body. That is why the first and most important learning in Ayurveda is to know our constitution or innate personality and then to create a lifestyle according to that personality. The following seven self-care steps takes us to the Naturality life.

Sleep:

Out of all the needs of the human body and mind, sleep is the most important one. We can live with inadequate food and exercise for months without serious damage to our body, but without optimal sleep the quality of life will deteriorate within a few days. During the night, we take a whole journey from the waking state to the dream state and then to dreamless sleep where we merge into the very source from where we emerged. Although we don't remember much of this, what we do experience in the morning is a sense of rejuvenation and energy. We feel ready for the challenges of the day. Disturbed sleep leave us tired, with less energy and poor decision-making capacities.

Yoga poses, breathing exercises and meditation practice makes the brain energized and the mind calmer. These effects are due to increasing blood flow to the brain and better connectivity within the various components of the brain. The result is a more harmonious and holistic functioning. If we don't have adequate sleep then this radical transformation of the brain may be disturbed, and we may not get the full benefit of our Naturality efforts. Only a few people are able to compensate for lost sleep through asanas, pranayama and meditation. Most have to make sure that they sleep well. Sleep and dream time can also be used for meditation practice.

Sleep helps us in:

- Healing and growth
- Rejuvenation of the immune, nervous, muscular and skeletal systems
- Memory processing: Working memory is important, because it keeps information active for further processing and supports higher-level cognitive functions such as decision making, reasoning, and episodic memory
- Dreams: Dreams are important symbols of our psycho-physical state. They not only give us a clue as to what is happening in our individual life, but they can connect to the *Sagun Braham* or universal consciousness, which is the common heritage of all humanity. Connecting to universal consciousness not only heals a person but takes them to higher states

of consciousness. The inner Guru is born out of these dream experiences, and we can be guided in our spiritual journey on a day-to-day basis. Dreams can also be a source of creativity. Many scientists, painters, writers and musicians got their inspiration from dreams. As a child, Albert Einstein had a dream that he was riding a sled down a steep, snowy slope, and as he approached the speed of light the colours all blended into one. This dream inspired him throughout his career to form his theories in physics. James Watson, one of the scientists who deciphered the structure of DNA, had a dream in which the shape of a double helix appeared in the form of a spiral staircase.

Food:

Food is the next important part of Naturality life. The doshas are connected with the digestive tract in a person. The stomach is connected with *Kapha* or earth, the small intestine with *Pitta* or fire and the large intestine with *Vata* or wind. In Ayurveda, doshas determine what type of food one should consume. The most important food caution is to eat less than a full stomach. As we mentioned earlier, the brain of a person on the path of Naturality needs more blood supply than a normal person, because the brain tissues are expanding and connecting with one another. Eating to the point of having a full stomach will divert the blood supply to the stomach rather than to the active brain, reducing the effect of the efforts.

Food should be fresh, warm, and vegetarian (unless adequate vegetarian food is not available or a person can't digest it). Food should be cooked properly and must not contain too many hot spices. Raw food is good only for few people or for a limited time period.

The human digestive tract contains the "gut brain," which has no cognitive capacity but has an ability to feel. Our gut brain gives a clear idea of the qualitative aspect (*Satvic*, *Rajsic*, and *Tamsic*) of food. Good food (Satvic) brings a sustained feeling of well-being, while Rajsic and Tamsic food may give transient pleasure but they are detrimental to one's well-being and nourishment in the long term. That is why we must think carefully about what kind of food we eat.

Exercise:

Neither the Asanas nor pranayama can replace a whole body workout. Exercise not only moves the muscles, joints, bones and organs to increase the blood perfusion, but it prevents brain aging and deterioration of memory. Brisk walking is the best exercise.

Relationships:

The most important relationship of a person on the path of Naturality is with himself/herself. Self-love and self-acceptance is the beginning of Naturality. Many reject this part of themselves and their bodies, because it's too painful to look at the dark parts of life. People label themselves as ugly and not worthy. They try to cope with self-rejection through mastering perfect poses or becoming a disciplinarian. Naturality involves following our own nature with ease and comfort. Unless we create a loving and harmonious relationship with ourselves, no matter what we do with our practice it won't come to fruition. Self-love is not self-indulgence or narcissism but rather self-care and self-respect. If we can love ourselves, we can love others without being pathologically attached or dependent on them. A lack of relationship with ourselves brings co-dependency and a lack of fulfilment.

Walking on the Naturality path doesn't mean dissolving our relationships with the world and living in isolation. We still remain connected to the world, but the centre of that connection is not in others; it is within ourselves. In other words, the centre of life is within rather than in the outside world.

Work:

To become a Natural doesn't mean that we stop working and expect the world to provide a livelihood for us. We have to fulfill our physical needs on our own. But this work must be according to our innate nature, which will enrich our practice. Most people's work is against their nature, and the work becomes a burden rather than a joy leading to fulfilment. Working according to our nature is Karma Yoga (Yoga of work). In Karma Yoga the work itself becomes an end rather than a means to some other end. It generates delight and is done without being attached to the fruit of the work. Work itself becomes fulfilment.

Home:

We don't need the help of a *Vastukala* or Feng Shui expert to build or arrange our home. Our home should be planned according to our dosha or personality. A Vata (Wind) person needs a small but cozy home with warm colors. A person with a Pitta (Fire) dosha must have a bigger house with cool colors and a Kapha (Earth)person's house must be free from darkness and humidity. The home should have just enough possessions for the need of the person.

Care of Others

Self-care is an essential first step on the path of Naturality, and care of others is equally important. Care of others begins with care of the family, and then this care extends to one's community, one's country, and the whole earth. Caring means to act with love and compassion in which we do not discriminate against others on the basis of ethnic background, religion, or class. This type of care is a complete action that not only serves others but it also benefits those who are serving. The server receives a sense of well-being, the love of others, prestige, and a healthy self-respect. The more we are connected to others, the more others will come to help us. It imparts to us a sense of fulfillment, meaning and purpose in life, and helps us to cope with loneliness, suffering and fear. A person who is connected to a family, society, country, and the earth develops a much broader vision and resilience to face life's storms.

In the beginning, the care of others may feel effortful, intentional, and perhaps inconvenient and uncomfortable. However, as the effort progresses, a point may come when this care of others becomes natural and fills both heart and mind with love and compassion. Now caring becomes second nature to the person, a spontaneous state of being in thoughts, in words and in actions.

As we share our material, mental and emotional resources, we help others to fulfill basic needs. Water to a thirsty person, food to the hungry, shelter to the homeless, education to the ignorant, and love and compassion to those experiencing fear and sorrow are some expressions of the ways we care for others. Caring also means to help maintain the laws which protect society from chaos and violence. It means that we do not participate in corrupt activities, and we do not hoard more than we need. Ultimately, caring for others is also care for oneself. Caring begins with an attitude of kindness and compassion towards one's own body, thoughts, and emotions.

Asanas, Pranayama and Meditation: All asanas, pranayama and meditations are not good for every dosha type. For Vata people, the asanas have to be simple and less strenuous, with *Ujjayi* pranayama and calming meditations. Prolonged chanting and singing may tire them. For people with a Pitta dosha, the same practices are good, but they can chant or sing for a longer period of time. People with a Kapha dosha need more stimulating yoga poses along with energetic pranayama such as *Kapalbhati*. Their meditation has to be dynamic, such as walking and dancing, and should involve other movement techniques and practices.

SELF-KNOWING: STUDYING THE BOOK OF LIFE

We accumulate vast amounts of knowledge over the course of our lives. We read constantly but the book that remains unread is the book of our own life. We don't realize that the source of all knowledge is the life that flows through us and through the universe. Science, religion and art all originate from this flow of life.

The book of life contains what was, what is and what will be. Without reading the book of life, our story can't be completed. We all have a story embedded in our biology and mind, but often it is interrupted by an endless parade of distractions, tragedies and losses. Unless we pick up the threads of our story we can't discover the meaning in our lives and discover our destiny.

In studying the book of our life, we must start with the conditioned brain and gradually move towards finding our innate nature. As we gain greater insight into our innate nature, the conditioning that stifles our personal growth begins to fall away. We begin to live with a more natural flow, a harmony of mind and body.

WORSHIP AND PRAYER

Worship and prayer emerge from the heart and are infused with love. Prayer transcends reason and calculation. It is the devotee's soulful expression of longing to see the Divine Beloved (God).

When prayer does find words, they are like mere waves on the surface of a vast ocean. Only the devotees' willingness to be thrown ever more deeply into the experience of prayer will lead them to a path previously unknown to them. It is this path, which is transparent and free from fear and guilt, that allows total surrender. This type of prayer is called worship. In this act of surrender, this worship, the devotee merges with the Divine Beloved.

Worship at this depth calls upon the devotee to journey inward into aloneness. No external teacher or guide is required. The heart becomes the guide, and without an intermediary, there is a direct connection with the Beloved.

Devotional Images on the Journey

Prayer is the heart's longing to unite and merge with the Divine. Usually, this prayer is focused on an image, idol or deity to which human-like qualities are attributed. Prayer cannot occur in a void or be offered to nothingness or the unknown. We need some image, whether it is of a god, goddess, prophet, ancestor, or elemental force to offer worship. Because these images are embedded in our subconscious, prayer is inwardly directed and fired by emotional energy.

Devotion is the force that guides prayer. A devotee is moved to pray by the desire to surrender to some higher presence. That complete surrender is an act of transcending the ego or limited self.

The path of meditation leads individuals to the same ego transcendence as the surrender of prayer. However, meditation takes the path of the intellect and is the silent, calm, non-judgmental witnessing of one's thoughts and mind. Dedicated devotion to the practice of meditation eventually throws us into the radical experience of ego-transcendence. We achieve a newfound clarity as well as a deep experience and comprehension of the wholeness of the internal and external worlds we inhabit.

Both in meditation and in prayer, it is the light of awareness that illuminates the dark corners of the mind and clears away the memories that clutter it. Shadows of these memories remain, but their emotional content is gone. The turmoil associated with them is also gone and we experience the freedom of true transcendence.

In meditation and in prayer we choose particular words, images and movements, organize them into a sequence, and perform them according to a plan. This mental and physical activity is clearly formulated by the mind, but it is the only way to begin on a deliberate path towards deeper awareness. The mind becomes a disciplined tool, which is necessary for us to move to the point of ego transcendence.

This explains why, in the beginning, meditation or prayer is mental, mechanical and repetitive. As we engage more deeply, the process becomes more organic, revealing the inner nature of the mind and its inherent vitality. We reach a breakthrough point after which meditation and prayer become spontaneous. We become meditative or prayerful all the time. In this state, life becomes an effortless meditation or prayer. The process continues without a conscious focus, whether we are eating, sleeping, working or making love.

We can see that meditation and prayer both begin with efforts of the will. In this way, meditation and prayer are similar to any other mental activity. Because our minds live within the confines of culture, religion and tradition, the first goal of meditation and prayer is to replace conventional religion and culture with our own way of thinking. Societal and cultural programming is a deep hypnotic spell under which individuals may spend years, never realizing that they are not living their true lives. When we decide to be hypnotized in our own way and through our own efforts, we begin the process of gaining control over ourselves.

PILGRIMAGE AND FASTING

PILGRIMAGE

"Travelling for transformation is pilgrimage."

Travel and pilgrimage are two different experiences. Travelling is movement for the sake of pleasure. While travelling, many people not only want to maintain the comfort and distractions they enjoy at home, but actually want more heightened experiences in a short period of time. They prefer not to stay long enough to develop an understanding of the place or people. A physical, emotional and intellectual status quo is maintained and there is little possibility for inner change during or after travel. Old boundaries stay intact and there is little inner growth.

Pilgrimage, on the other hand, is movement in order to challenge the ego or self, physically, emotionally and intellectually. Pilgrimage is done with humility and with an open mind. We prepare to face the unknown. Pilgrimage puts a strain on the individual, which may lead to a point where old boundaries and limits are broken. This brings about change, transformation and the emergence of a new layer of self or a deeper and broader self. This may lead to the union of the body and mind (emotions, intellect) and subsequently to the discovery of the soul (mind-body integration).

FASTING

There are two reasons to engage in fasting. The first reason to fast is to withdraw from what we don't need. Every day we consume an excess of food, water, space, energy and wealth. This overconsumption inevitably creates problems—for ourselves, for others, and for the environment in which we live. When we learn to live in a naturally austere way, we lessen the burden on others and on our planet. Also, we feel lighter and healthier, consuming only what we need.

The second reason for fasting is to withdraw from food and water for a short period of time to eliminate toxins and unburden the body. Such fasting helps to break the comfortable but confining boundaries we have been accustomed to since birth. Fasting has the same effect as pilgrimage. It brings new insight and breaks the structure of the old self so that we can experience a new dimension of living.

If our body gets cold, the mind takes it as a sign of impending death. If our breathing becomes subtle, that too is taken as a sign of approaching death and we experience fear. In the same way, if food is withdrawn from the body, the mind takes it as an indication of famine and we experience the fear of death. That is why fasting (withdrawal from solid food, while continuing with fluids) is a good way to gain some insight into the process of dying. It is a safe way to come to terms with mortality.

During fasting, the body experiences hunger and unpleasant sensations. However, after three to four days of restlessness and stress, hunger disappears and the body starts living off its own resources. In the beginning, the mind is anxious and fearful but gradually it becomes calm and merges into the witnessing self.

Fasting can take us to the witnessing self, a state in which joy, energy and calmness are simultaneously present. The emergence of the witnessing self is the beginning of coming to terms with our own mortality. A body that is fasting activates itself and the brain to create a pain-free, calm and high-energy state. This is the result of neurochemicals such as endorphins, dopamine, nor-epinephrine and serotonin pouring into the brain and body. If the body's functioning is not interfered with by too many medical procedures and medications, this state can also be an experience of the dying process.

Death is an integral part of the body and the body has sufficient resources to deal with it in a smooth and orderly way. However, when the mind interferes too much in the process, death becomes a frightening experience. Controlled, supervised fasting is a way to counteract this and to let the mind experience and prepare for the process of dying. Fasting should be done in a natural, restful and conflict-free environment, where a guide is present. Chanting, meditation, prayer and worship are positive additions to the process.

YOGA

Yoga brings the following benefits:

- **Full orientation of the body in space and time.** This brings about a state of balance, which enhances body awareness. The body learns to move naturally and without fear.

- **Moving from body image to the body-actual.** Our body image is created by our cultural memories and beliefs and does not represent the real body. Many mind-body pathologies are the result of our body image. The body-actual is the body's map in the brain and represents the real body. To live in the body-actual is to ground the awareness in reality and create stability.

- **Mind-body integration.** Paying attention to body postures brings the mind and body together. Normally our mind is absorbed in thinking and is distracted while the body is in action.

- **Neuro-vascular stimulation.** Holding a body posture for a sustained period of time stimulates neuro-vascular bundles in the body, which are rich in sympathetic and parasympathetic nerves. During a yoga pose, the pressure on specific parts of the body stimulates neurovascular bundles and plexuses. This leads to relaxation because of decreased activity in the sympathetic nervous system and an increased activation of the parasympathetic nervous system. The brain, immune and endocrine systems begin to function at their optimum, creating mind-body homeostasis, which is experienced as a sense of well-being.

- **Healing.** Poses and movements release embedded memories of abuse, trauma and pain and heal the body and mind.

Yoga poses were not invented by a specific person in a particular time and place. They developed from the observation that when we experience inner states such as fear, anger, peace, joy and tranquility, the body moves in a particular way. A joyful child may begin to dance spontaneously. If we are sad, we may also be able to experience joy if we dance. Happiness brings a natural smile but if we smile intentionally it may give us a feeling of happiness. Laughter yoga is based on this observation. Great actors know this and produce expressions at will by changing their breathing and taking specific body postures. It follows that if we intentionally move in a certain way or take a certain pose, we create specific inner states in the body. This is the law of "Reciprocal Response."

Consciously maintaining a certain pose also gives us a more accurate orientation of the body in space, which generates better balance, grounds the mind in the body and improves its overall functioning. This is the result of right hemispheric stimulation, which has a calming effect and also increases creativity and hemispheric synchronization. Also, the brain develops a more accurate map of the body and is able to work in harmony with it.

In the beginning, yoga poses and movements are intentional but a point comes when they become spontaneous. Our inner state guides the body to assume certain postures that allow for a smooth, unobstructed flow of energy.

In order to optimize the benefits of yoga, the following guidelines should be observed:

- Poses should be sustained for varying lengths of time, depending on an individual's flexibility and endurance. The minimum duration is twenty seconds.
- At no point should we hold our breath.
- Individuals should remain aware of the pose and/or breath.
- Opposite poses complement each other and bring balance.
- One should not feel tired after yoga poses.

NATURALITY YOGA POSES

Naturality poses are not rigid in nature. They can be done either standing, sitting or lying down. When practicing Naturality poses, the body is allowed to take any posture that is comfortable and pleasant. Through stretching, some tension is brought to the pose. The pose is maintained for a few minutes with full breath and attention.

Naturality poses are good for anyone, particularly for the elderly, handicapped, and those living with chronic pain, disease or general stiffness.

Sai Yoga:

Sai Yoga is the combination of prayer poses from different religious traditions of the world. It is named after the great universal spiritual teacher Shirdi Sai Baba. A guide to this particular set of poses is as follows:

1. Stand and spread the arms in an opening and receiving pose, with the neck extended and the gaze directed upwards.

2. Stand straight and let the folded hands rest on the heart center in the middle of the chest.

3. Bend forward at the waist, palms resting on the knees.

4. Kneel and let folded hands rest on the heart center in the middle of the chest.

5. Sit on heels, hands on knees and allow the forehead to touch the ground three times.

6. Lie prostrate (face down) with folded hands fully stretched forward above the head.

7. Raise head; let folded hands rest on the forehead. Now reverse the process by coming into a seated position on your heels and going back through the poses to the first pose.

Full breathing continues during the poses. Prayer or chanting may be done at the same time as the poses, if desired.

Sleep Pose:

Sleep pose is the posture we take when preparing for sleep. It helps in preserving energy and maintains calmness during sleep.

Lying on our right side is best because it allows breathing to occur through the left nostril. Left nostril breathing stimulates the right side of the brain, which brings calmness and silence as it is the left brain that is connected with thoughts. This position also encourages gastric emptying. In sleep pose, the legs are crossed at the ankle or shin, and the hands are folded as in prayer. This allows the body's energy to flow in a circle and without any wastage of it.

BINDU (POINT) YOGA:

Point or Bindu yoga poses press and activate some of the major energy points in the body. This brings vitality and relieves stress and pain, particularly in the head and face area. This sequence of poses begins with a series of standard yoga poses, whose description can be found in any book about yoga. Following these standard poses, there is a sequence of poses aimed at pressing specific energy points on the body.

Begin by standing in Mountain pose.

1. Move smoothly into Cat pose.

2. Next, lie prostrate with your folded hands fully stretched forward.

3. Raise your head and press the seven bindus or pressure points as follows:
    - Middle of the forehead
    - Eyebrows
    - Temple
    - TMJ or temporal-mandibular joint where the ear joins the face
    - Cheek bone
4. Now, place your chin in your cupped palms, and use your thumbs to knuckle the inner sides of your eyes
5. Come back into Cat pose
6. Move smoothly into Child's pose
7. Finally, end the sequence in Mountain pose

Full breathing has to be maintained throughout the poses, along with body awareness.

BREATHING OR PRANAYAMA

KALAJAYI BREATH OR THE BREATH OF DISSOLUTION

There are many different breathing techniques that can be practiced. Which technique is most effective depends on the individual. Kalajayi breathing or breath of dissolution is based on a new breathing technique. *Kalajayi* comes from two words, *Kaal* = "death" or "time" and *Jayi* = "becoming victorious." Kalajayi is a breathing technique used to overcome the fear of death.

Breathing is a unique phenomenon in humans because of its involuntary and voluntary aspects. First of all, breathing happens in the present, so whatever we do with the breath is going to be connected with the present moment. Secondly, breathing is a bridge between the body and mind and so it changes when we experience different mental and emotional states. If we are calm, breathing is deep and slow. If we feel a sense of love, our breathing becomes deep and slow. In anger, the breath is deep and fast, while in fear, it is shallow and rapid. In extreme fear, we hold our breath. Thirdly, breathing is partly involuntary and partly voluntary, which means that we can partially control it to achieve certain body-mind states.

When death is approaching, our breathing pattern takes a distinct form. Our breathing is deeper and faster with progressively more forceful exhalations. This reaches a peak and then breathing becomes shallow and eventually stops for a few moments. This cycle is repeated. This type of breathing pattern is called Cheyne-Stokes respiration.

The Technique:

Kalajayi breathing can be practiced either lying down or sitting comfortably in a chair. After closing the eyes and relaxing for a few seconds, allow the breath to become progressively deeper and faster while the exhalations becomes longer and longer. After three such deep inhalations and deeper exhalations, take three progressively shallower breathes and then suspend the breath completely for a few seconds before breathing normally again.

A single cycle of Kalajayi is composed of six breaths or six inhalations and exhalations.

- First breath is normal
- Second is deeper and faster, with a longer exhale
- Third is deepest, with the longest exhale
- Fourth is slightly less deep
- Fifth is shallower and slower, similar to second

- Sixth is normal
- Brief pause

Repeat this cycle. In the beginning (in a single sitting) individuals should not do more than three to five cycles. Later on, when one is more comfortable with this breathing technique, the number of cycles can be increased.

Kalajayi breath helps in reducing the thoughts or may bring a single thought state.

MEDITATION

Meditation is the de-conditioning of the brain and body. It is relaxation, awareness and expansion of awareness. The word meditation comes from the Latin root *meditatum*, which means "to ponder." *Dhyana* comes from the Sanskrit root *dhyai*, meaning to "contemplate" or "meditate." It also means attention. Meditation can help to shatter the prison of conditioning, allowing us to emerge into a new state of being.

THE HISTORY OF MEDITATION

It is not certain when the practice of meditation actually began. Perhaps it started with the first humans on earth as they naturally experienced various states of altered consciousness. Later on, it became an essential practice that shamans, healers and priests used to communicate with spirits and dead ancestors.

Meditation was a part of the pre-Vedic and Vedic tradition in India and techniques of meditation were described more than 5000 years ago. It is an integral part of all Indian religions and practices. The most definitive book about meditation, *Vigyan Bhairava Tantra*, is four thousand years old. It is a dialogue between Siva and his consort Devi, in which Siva describes 112 meditation techniques to Devi.

It is important to note that a **meditation technique is NOT meditation.** However, meditation techniques are important ways to calm the mind and bring many other benefits to body and emotional states.

ACTIVE AND RECEPTIVE MEDITATIONS

Active meditation techniques integrate body movements and breathing exercises.

Receptive meditation is masterly inactivity, or in other words a calm observation of what is going on. Vipassana or Mindfulness and Zazen are examples of receptive meditation.

WITNESSING AND ABSORPTIVE MEDITATION

In witnessing meditation such as Mindfulness, the meditator is alert, attentive, calm and doesn't lose consciousness.

In absorptive meditation, the meditator is totally absorbed by the meditative experience and may lose body consciousness. Kirtan and whirling dance are examples of absorptive meditation.

In the following section, two new meditation techniques will be introduced.

BRAHAM OR EXPANSIVENESS MEDITATION

Braham is a Sanskrit noun, which is derived from the verb *Briha*, which means "expansive" or "vast." Sometimes it is equated to the word "God," but in its original sense, the word means "the ever-expanding awareness which includes all that is possible and all that exists." It includes the Becoming and the Being. It is both time and space as well as that which is beyond time and space.

The brain has no perceptual boundaries and can focus on a dewdrop or on a remote galaxy in the immensity of space. It can go back and forth between the states of Being and Becoming with ease. But when the ego or the self, which consists of thought, breaks the intimacy between the brain and the biological universe, we become confined by mental space and time. We are trapped in a world of names and forms, and suffer from fear, conflict and discontent.

Labeling our world is essential to create order. However, when labeling carries a judgment such as good and bad, inferior and superior, ugly and beautiful or right and wrong it creates division, fragmentation and conflict. The same applies to form. We create a mental map (form) of what is desirable, pleasurable and familiar. What is outside of these things is excluded from that mental map. This also leads to fragmentation and distortion.

The purpose of Braham or Expansiveness Meditation is to expand the boundaries of consciousness and to eventually break them. This allows the brain to become free to experience unbound perception. In the process of expansion, the brain begins to include even that which is not familiar, desirable or pleasant in its field of consciousness. As a result, fear and hostility dissipate as our sense of rigid "otherness" disappears. All becomes a part of the one, non-dual movement of life. It is a state of peace, passion and bliss, free from fear, conflict and discontent.

The Technique:

1. Begin with slow, deep and gentle belly breathing for five minutes.

2. With closed eyes, feel the whole body, not focusing on any particular body part. Feel the presence of the body. This establishes awareness of your own presence. Stay with it for five minutes.

3. Allow your relaxed awareness (and/or body) to expand slowly three to four feet around you. Notice what you hear, see and feel. Stay with it for five minutes.

4. Expand your awareness further in all directions until it fills the space you occupy (room, studio, etc). Whatever comes into this field of expanded awareness becomes a part of you. People, objects, buildings, sounds, light and any elements of nature—all become part of your awareness. Thoughts, memories and emotions are also part of your awareness. They are not separate from you. They are part of your being. Stay with this for five minutes.

5. Allow your awareness to expand further until it no longer has a distinct boundary.

6. Stay with it for five minutes.

7. Slowly allow your field of awareness to shrink back to your own body's presence.

8. Open your eyes.

Alternative Technique: The following technique can be used to create a similar experience.

1. Bring a relaxed focus to the middle of the chest. Slowly bring this focus into the darkness of the heart space deep within the chest for 2- 3 minutes.

2. Become aware of the breath in the darkness of the heart space for -minutes.

3. Allow the breath to slow and deepen without strain. Slow, deep inhalation and slow, deep exhalation, for minutes.

4. Allow breathing to return to normal and regular for - minutes.

5. Visualize, imagine or feel a flame or light with a warm glow deep in the heart space. Allow it to occur without forcing it. Be open. Continue for minutes.

6. Let that warm glow slowly fill the body from within, starting from the head, and then moving to the eyes, face, neck, shoulders, chest, left upper limb, right upper limb, belly, pelvic area and buttocks, left lower limb and right lower limb. The whole body glows with a warm light.

7. Let go of any images and simply become aware of sensations and feelings. You are feeling your own presence.

8. Allow the feeling of your warm and glowing presence to spread beyond the boundary of the body to two feet around it.

9. Allow it to expand further and fill the whole room. The whole room is filled with your own presence and whatever comes into the field of your presence and awareness becomes part of you.

10. Allow it to expand further beyond the room and go wherever it goes, without any limit.

11. Then allow your presence and awareness to shrink to the room.

12. Gradually become aware of your body.

13. Take three deep breaths and slowly open your eyes.

NEH OR SELF–LOVE MEDITATION

The world is a projection of the mind. If we are sad the world looks sad, and if we are happy the world feels like a happy place. If we are full of fear then people, places and events bring fear into our hearts, and if we are without fear, we experience freedom everywhere. We each have our own heaven and hell within and we project them onto the world around us. A sunset may be beautiful for someone experiencing joy within, while the same sunset may be sad for someone who has just lost a loved one.

The same is true for love. If we love ourselves, then the world is full of love. If we are hateful or fearful of our own bodies, emotions and thoughts, it is difficult to love others. We project the rejection and resentment that we feel for ourselves onto our surroundings. We may act as if we love others. We may even have convinced ourselves of this love, but such love does not emerge from the depths of our heart. It is merely the fulfillment of a need, or a social formality. We may use the word love but it doesn't carry the energy of true intimacy.

Neh means "affection" or "love." This meditation is about loving our bodies, feelings, emotions and thoughts and expressing that affection toward ourselves. It is simply not possible to learn to love ourselves through a meditation technique. However, although the practice of meditation can't create love, it can uncover love that is hidden deep within us. Love is an essential component of physical and psychological well-being. It is always there, but it may be buried beneath layers of social, cultural and religious conditioning.

Self-Love is not selfishness. It is not self-indulgence or narcissistic attachment to, or obsession with, our body or mind. In narcissism, the absorption or attachment with the self is so great that we become oblivious to the needs and desires of others. People become merely tools for self-gratification. A narcissistic person lives in isolation away from the world and nature.

Rarely do we love ourselves totally. Sometimes we are attached to ourselves and become self-absorbed. Often we don't like or may even hate ourselves. We repress or ignore those parts of our being, which we feel are unworthy and ugly. This results in a fragmented self. Instead of feeling an integrated wholeness within, we divide ourselves into the "good" and "bad." These parts are in constant conflict with each other. The "bad" is repressed, ignored and rejected by the "good."

Neh meditation is a technique of non-judgmental loving of all parts of the self, including the physical, emotional and thought components. Such an act of loving is a movement from fragmentation to wholeness, from self-hatred and guilt to affection, and from a manufactured self-image to living with reality. It is an action towards total self-acceptance, in which one lives without guilt.

If we love ourselves and feel affection towards our body, feelings and thoughts, love and affection will fill the vessel of our body and mind. This love will spill into the world around us. If we go into Neh meditation with our whole heart and energy, the technique will become our nature. In such a transformation, self-love and self-affection become love and affection for others, the world and all of creation.

The Technique:

Sitting comfortably in a chair or on the floor, remember moments when your body and mind were filled with love and affection. You are not an observer of these moments but are re-living them. Feel the love and affection you had in those moments, here and now throughout your being.

1. Allow that love and affection to fill you and flow from your head to your toes.

   This feeling of love and affection is filling your:

   - head space, eyes, face, jaw, mouth, ear, neck, chest, abdomen
   - left shoulder, upper arm, elbow, forearm, wrist, hand, fingers and thumb

- right shoulder, upper arm, elbow, forearm, wrist, hand, thumb and fingers. First on the left side, then the right side.
- upper, middle and lower back, pelvic area
- left hip, thigh, knee, leg, ankle, foot and toes
- right hip, thigh, knee, leg, ankle, foot and toes

2. Remember any words, sounds, fragrances, tastes and touch that were present in those moments where you experienced the power of love.

3. Allow your whole being to merge into that feeling of love.

4. Now feel the energy of love and affection in your body, particularly in the area of your heart.

5. Allow the energy in your body and heart to flow towards your hands, fingers and thumbs. Your hands, fingers and thumbs are vibrating with that loving energy.

6. With your hands, fingers and thumbs, slowly and tenderly touch, and gently press:

    - the sides of your head, eyes, face, jaw and ears
    - your neck, shoulders, upper arm, elbows, forearm, hands, fingers and thumbs
    - your chest, abdomen, pelvic area
    - your thighs, knee, legs, ankle, feet and toes
    - the parts of your back accessible to you
    - your first chakra at the base of your spine
    - your second chakra just above your pubic bone
    - your third chakra at your naval area
    - your fourth chakra in the middle of your chest
    - your fifth chakra at the root of your neck
    - your sixth chakra in the middle of two eyebrows
    - your seventh chakra on the top of your head

- your emotions and thoughts

7. Now cross your arms reaching for opposite shoulders and hug yourself.

8. Lie down for five to ten minutes and acknowledge all your feelings.

The same meditation can be done if you are healing or sending love to another person.

DREAM AND SLEEP MEDITATION

It is possible to continue one's meditation practice even during the night, during the sleeping and dreaming states. In fact, night is the best time to meditate because we are not engaged in any other activity except resting in bed. Also, there is another advantage to meditating in the night. We don't need to worry about our body or the controlling "I" that prevents us from going into deeper layers of our own being and consciousness. During sleep, we are free from the limitations of the body and that superficial controlling "I."

We can think about the stages of sleep from the point of view of brain evolution. As we fall asleep, our consciousness descends from the neo-cortex to the mammalian brain, where visual images dominate, giving rise to dreams. From the mammalian brain, consciousness descends to the reptilian brain, where the silence of the deep sleep is experienced.

But how do we meditate during the states of sleep and dreaming? We must first prepare the brain during the day, by constantly reminding ourselves that whatever we are experiencing within and outside in the world are like dreams. We really don't understand the reality of the outside world. If we ask scientists, they will tell us that the universe is energy and when that energy interacts with our eyes, ears, tongue, skin or nose, our mind creates experience. That experience depends upon our memories and our memories are conditioned by our past. For example, consider a tree or flower in the outside world. The idea and image of the tree or flower is created by our sense perception. If we practice thinking of the world as a dream, this will become a conscious pointer during the night. When the experience goes deep enough, then we will become progressively more conscious, initially during the dream state and later during deep sleep.

The sleep and dream state, the meditative state and the experience of dying have the same stages, although the intensity with which we experience them is different. Sleep is the least and dying is the most intense experience. In all three states, consciousness goes through waking, dreaming or visual imagery, followed by an imageless silence.

There is another difference between these three experiences. Meditation is conscious, while in the states of sleep/dream and of dying we don't remain conscious unless meditation becomes seamlessly incorporated into them. If we continue to develop our meditative practice, we can become conscious even during sleeping and dreaming. As we develop this consciousness, we realize that every night we take a great journey which takes us from the waking consciousness to the soul, from soul to universal mind or God and from there to the non-dual state in which silence is experienced. The last state is called *Turiya* or simply, "the fourth state." As we become more meditative, even dying becomes a conscious phenomenon, and becomes merely a bridge between this life and the life beyond the body's death.

In other words, our ordinary mind divides the waking state from the dream state and deep sleep, but actually there are no divisions. An analogy would be the way we draw national boundaries on earth. When we look at the earth from outer space, we realize that there are no boundaries but a vast expanse of nature in different forms, without any defining lines to divide them. Once we realize and feel the fact of undivided consciousness, we become more aware during the dream state and deep sleep. We may then experience all the stages of meditation in a single night.

The Technique

Dream and sleep meditation technique has four parts to it.

1. **Sleep pose:** Sleep pose is the posture we take when preparing for sleep. It helps in preserving energy and maintaining calmness during sleep.

   Lying on our right side is best because it allows breathing to occur through the left nostril. Left nostril breathing stimulates the right side of the brain, which brings calmness and silence as it is the left brain that is connected with thoughts. This position also encourages gastric emptying. In sleep pose, the legs are crossed at the ankle or shin, and the hands are folded as in prayer. This allows the body's energy to flow in a continuous circle, without wastage.
   We can experiment with taking this pose and see if we can sleep comfortably in this way. If it doesn't feel comfortable, then we can take any other pose that feels natural for us.

2. **Letting go of the day:** In this step, we remember the day that has just passed, in as much detail as we can—visual images, feelings, touch, smell, taste and sounds. We do this mindfully and slowly, rewinding the day starting from the last event of the day and reaching to the point where we just woke up from sleep in the morning. During this rewinding, we focus on letting go of the emotionally significant events. We can repeat this process of rewinding two to three times, to make sure that we let go of most of the emotional experiences of the day. This allows us to enter into the night without stress, worry and conflict.

3. **Deep breathing:** After letting go, take deep breaths to relax the body and mind.

4. **Light in the heart:** Visualize, imagine or feel a flame or light at a point between the eyebrows. Slowly allow that flame to descend along the midline of the nose, lips, chin and neck, until it is established deep in the heart space in the middle of the chest. By gently focusing on this light, we slip into sleep.

This last step is done to bring our consciousness down from the thinking mind to the feeling heart.

Chapter 7

EXPERIENCES ON THE PATH OF NATURALITY, PART 1: THE EGO AND BEYOND

The first step on the path of Naturality is the development of a healthy ego. Without a well-grounded ego, the foundations of spiritual life will be shaky. If we attempt to transcend an ego that is not fully formed, we can face both mental and physical health problems.

THE HEALTHY EGO

The four features of a healthy ego are as follows:

1. Self-care
2. Care of others
3. Trust
4. Boundaries

1. SELF-CARE

Self-care and self-love are the most important features of a healthy ego. If we can love and take care of ourselves, then we can do the same for others. Self-care includes care of the body, emotions and intellect, which leads to growth and development. Self-care should be done according to our innate nature.

2. CARE OF OTHERS

Care of others is not only needed to ward off self-indulgence and narcissism, but also to maintain one's self-esteem, which is the ego's driving force. In a way, appropriate care of others is equivalent to self-care. An ego shaped by culture needs energy and rewards from family and society. It is through the care of others that we receive these rewards.

3. TRUST

When we have a healthy ego, we are able to trust people. These bonds of trust promote psychological health, and they also help us move ahead in the world. Forging strong links with others will support us in times of both prosperity and hardship. Without this vital trust, we will live in constant anxiety and sense danger everywhere.

4. BOUNDARIES

When we have a healthy ego, we also need to create boundaries. Appropriate boundaries protect us from others who might harm us physically or emotionally. The concept of boundaries also applies to our own mental landscape. We can't allow all of the endless thoughts and emotions that arise within us to occupy our brain, or else our emotional landscape will be in chaos. We must learn the art of discriminating between what is healthy and appropriate for us, and what is harmful. We must allow in only that which can be assimilated with ease and comfort. It can be tempting to leave ourselves wide open to all sorts of people, experiences, thoughts and emotions—but this is not healthy. Creating boundaries is the art of saying "No."

INDIVIDUAL AND COLLECTIVE EGO

The ego not only provides protection from the maddening dance of life and death but it also helps in survival, both individually and collectively. At an individual level, a well-developed ego is an essential step on our life's journey. As we explored earlier in this chapter, the healthy ego has four elements: self-care, care of others, trust, and boundaries. These form a solid foundation for the development of the personality and a well-functioning social identity. Without this foundation, an individual who tries to explore the mysteries of life and death may be thrown into emotional chaos.

At a collective level, ego consciousness makes humans a self-reflective species, aware of the vast movement of emotions, thoughts and memory. As this awareness develops, we can reflect upon life and decide the course of action that is best for our survival and development. We move to a level of reflection that helps us to prevent actions that put our lives at risk. Because of this capacity for awareness, reflection and planned action, we have become the most powerful species on earth.

But what are the costs of this dominance of ego in our lives? The ego is like an engine that constantly needs fuel to operate. Self-esteem is this fuel. Without constant injections of self-esteem, the ego collapses. Self-esteem is boosted by rewards, achievements and recognition. Elaborate social and cultural traditions, customs and behaviours constantly create the energy of self-esteem. While this is a natural and positive process, we can become slaves to our egos, caught up in an endless cycle of seeking approval and reward.

Our ego has been strongly influenced by the process of enculturation, creating a worldview whose boundaries are limited by a particular place and time. Also, our experiences are being constantly filtered by the ego, allowing in only those perceptions that do not shake an artificially created sense of security. The combination of these factors results in a narrow and distorted view of the world.

The protective boundaries imposed by the ego also block us from fully experiencing who we are. By confining reality to symbols, we gain some sense of mastery over our environment. But in the process of naming the nameless, life becomes trapped by symbols and its free movement is lost within the rigid boundary of form. Instead of intimacy with a world teeming with life, we experience only a partial view of the world, limited by the boundaries created by our symbols. We have to go beyond these boundaries in order to experience life and death directly.

LEARNING ABOUT OUR OWN EGOS: AN EGO TYPOLOGY

Learning more about the characteristics of own egos can be very helpful in our quest to discover our innate nature. Thousands of years ago, Indian sages and Ayurvedic scholars developed a typology of the ego, which can serve as a basis for examination of our own ego tendencies. In this typology of the ego, there are three categories:

1. **Tamsic or stuck/inert**: People in whom this type of constitution is predominant are fearful, and avoid action in the world. Often, they suffer from low self-esteem. The thought of action brings anxiety. As a result, their motivation to move forward in the world is lacking.

2. **Rajsic or passionate**: A person with a Rajsic ego tends to be assertive, arrogant and sometimes aggressive. Such individuals are often thought to be egotistic. On the positive side, these

individuals are active in the world, and may display significant leadership qualities.

3. **Satvic or harmonious:** People in whom a Satvic ego is predominant tend to be caring, gentle and loving. The Satvic ego is the most adaptable ego type, and such individuals often are naturally drawn to a spiritual path.

OPENING THE DOOR TO SELF-KNOWING: THE WAY OF CRISIS AND LOSS

Most people prefer to stay within the familiar boundaries of their known world—a comfortable place for the ego. However, sometimes life will impart them a shattering blow, whether it is a personal loss, a failure, or a devastating illness. This event destroys the edifice upon which the ego is built. In such moments, the ego's comfortable world crumbles. These catastrophic moments in life allow the suppressed content of the subconscious to flood the mind, brain and body. We become overwhelmed and lost. We feel a sense of disillusionment as we realize that the social and cultural values we held dear are limited and give us no real understanding of life. Once this devastating realization sets in, we may fall into despair.

For most people, recovery from a devastating life event involves rebuilding the structure of the ego. We try to incorporate the event into the way we view the world, by making it a part of the narrative of our life. This is a healthy strategy in many ways, because it allows us to begin functioning in the world once more. However, by merely rebuilding the structure of the ego we are actually losing a precious opportunity for spiritual growth.

In order for us to progress spiritually beyond the bounds of the ego's structure, we have to face our subconscious. Conscious life is only a small part of our total existence. It's like the tip of the iceberg, while hidden underneath is a vast ocean of human experience. Here lie feelings of guilt, anger, and fear; memories of trauma, failure and despair; wounds and scars from painful events of the past. But this mysterious ocean of human experience also includes light, insight, creativity and joy—the most precious gifts of the subconscious. These treasures can be discovered when we enter the dark world of the subconscious and illuminate it with the light of consciousness. We can then transform its energy and integrate it into our daily lives.

So we see that a shattering experience of disillusionment can actually become the catalyst for great spiritual growth. We become vulnerable and receptive, acquiring the sensitivity required for change. When we reach this level of sensitivity, then the distraction and protection provided by the ego is no longer effective. If this process is allowed to take its own course, it leads to the experience of soul or wholeness. A second birth occurs within us as we are born into the wholeness of soul. We become creators and recreate ourselves. Rebirth is the result of this mind-body union.

OPENING THE DOOR TO SELF-KNOWING: THE WAY OF LOVE

Love cannot dissolve the ego but it provides space and is a catalyst for such dissolution. Although love helps us cope with fear, it cannot take us beyond it. However, it provides the ground upon which fearlessness can develop.

Love is "hard wired" into the body and brain. This feeling we call love is a deep part of all living beings, an essential condition for survival. Out of love, new life is conceived and born. Out of love, a mother cares for her child. Feelings of love are present at all levels of human relationship, whether it is between a parent and child, between lovers, wife and husband, brother and sister or between friends. This love has nothing to do with a conscious cultivation of the emotion of affection. It is simply present in the fibres of all living beings. Love expresses itself in many forms depending on the stage of evolution. It can manifest as sex, passion, emotional attachment, devotion, intellectual longing and universal love or connection.

Not only does love have a basic survival value, it is essential for pleasure, joy and wellness in daily life. Babies who are not touched in a loving way during the early months of their lives suffer from an inner atrophy. Their brains do not mature fully and they miss something vital for proper development. They may look physically healthy but their inner world doesn't have the same richness of feeling and response. They may be emotionally cold and are often unable to form lasting bonds. They may lose their capacity to receive and give love, and as a result experience loneliness. We cannot live without pleasure, so if deprived, we seek pleasure through food, power, wealth, dominance and excessive consumption.

Real love not only gives us freedom from those complex systems of pleasure but also cultivates a natural restraint. A person who experiences love derives contentment from within by connecting lovingly with others. Such contentment prevents the search for excessive external pleasure. Love gives us a feminine or nurturing quality, and a gentle flexibility expresses itself within us. Loving people don't seek worldly power for their own gain and they are not empire-builders. At some level, it is a lack of love that pushes us to consume, dominate and kill. We may become materially rich but remain poor, lonely and insecure within.

Although each cell of our body is soaked with love, we don't always perceive that love. So often, these feelings are obscured and suppressed by the thinking mind. As time goes on, the mind's presence becomes more and more overwhelming and slowly love becomes a thought process. However, if love is given its full expression, then it can break through the rigidity of the mind, and wash away all the structures created by thought. Love clears the path for a sacred journey.

When the body discovers its innate love, the prison of the ego is shattered. Love unleashes energy in the very root of our being, uncovering hidden memories of trauma, tragedies and conditioning. Because it washes away the past and awakens the body, love provides space for true revolution and real reformation. The body's awakening is a biological transformation that soaks our whole being with unending passion.

As love ascends from the lower levels it becomes progressively freer. It moves from sex to attachment, attachment to devotion, devotion to creativity and finally from creativity to bliss. When love surpasses its own limits, it becomes nameless and timeless.

EGO, FREE WILL AND FREEDOM

As we develop a more scientific understanding of our world and of our own body and mind, it is becoming clear that there are no independent entities, individuals or even thoughts in the universe. Everything is connected with everything else. Since every part of nature affects and influences every other part, there is no possibility of complete independence.

This brings us to the question of *free will*. Free will is the ability to think and act completely independent of our environment or culture. A person with free will can live in absolute aloneness and act on the world with total freedom.

But is free will really possible?

We are not born as clean slates. We come into the world with our own particular nature, constitution or temperament, which determines how we are going to respond to the natural and human-made world. The blueprint of future behaviour has been laid down even before we are born. Our nature is not rigid, however, because it contains a range of possibilities. It is the foundation upon which we build our lives. This nature is the result of countless past generations and their interaction with the environment. This is all transmitted through our parents' genes.

After birth, culture begins to condition us to become people who can be assimilated and absorbed into society. In essence, a person is a product of both their genetic makeup and cultural conditioning. While genes create a general biological and psychological template, cultural and social influences fill in the specific details of the person. This mixture of nature and nurture forms the basic structure of the ego.

Is it therefore possible to think of a person as someone with free will? Can we become totally independent of the world and think, speak, choose and act completely free of any internal or external influence whatsoever? *Free will is neither biologically nor psychologically possible.* Free will is an illusion of the ego, a false understanding of the importance of the individual self within the universe. With the increasing dominance of ego in our lives, we forget our original nature. We use the ego as a shield against the fear of death, and gradually we live our lives within that illusory world. Instead of being a shield to protect us from fear, the ego becomes a prison that traps us and prevents us from perceiving a greater truth.

The illusory world creates by the ego is shattered when death comes to the physical body, because the ego is rendered helpless and eventually, it collapses. But is it possible to move out of that illusory world before we face our physical death? In other words, is it possible to transcend the ego?

GOING BEYOND THE EGO

We have seen that the idea of free will actually isolates us from the rest of the world. If we truly had free will, we could act independently of the past and future. But this is simply not possible. As we develop a more scientific understanding of our world and of our own body and mind, it is becoming clear that there are no independent entities, individuals or even thoughts in the universe. Everything is connected with everything else. Since every part of nature affects and influences every other part, there is no possibility of complete independence and therefore, we cannot have true free will. Instead, we must see the universe as a whole, wherein each part is integral to the whole.

However, the absence of free will doesn't mean the absence of freedom. Life always gives us many choices, and there are many doors to freedom waiting to be opened. We can think of life as having a wide range of possibility, which may become reality as our awareness expands. With this expanding awareness, one becomes cognizant of the presence of the many doors to freedom—doors that were always there but hidden. As we learn to open these doors, we move into greater awareness and a different quality of freedom.

This freedom is part of a wholeness that goes beyond an ego trapped by ignorance. As we make a choice on the path to freedom, a new door opens. This gives us more freedom and more choice. Finally, a point comes when this freedom becomes boundless, timeless and infinite. At that point all doors disappear and no structure confines life. This is the experience of a cosmic state. Here, there is no free will but total freedom.

CONNECTION OF EGO WITH THE FOUR ASHRAMS (OR STAGES) OF LIFE

In Indian philosophy, human life is a harmonious functioning of four stages or Ashrams: *Brahamcharya* or the stage of learning, *Grihastha* or the stage of householder, *Vanprastha* or the stage of exploration and adventure and *Sanyasa*, the stage of seeking liberation and preparing for death.

The ashram system indicates that life is like the flow of a river, fluid and ever-changing. If we align ourselves with that flow, we live fully. If we do not do this, we become stagnant - prisoners of the past. Instead of a free flowing river, life becomes like the stale water of a pool that gradually dries up. These four stages of life merge into each other seamlessly. As we move through these stages of life, we fulfill the needs of society at the same time as we grow and develop as individuals. Thus, this natural, stage-by-stage process includes both the harmonious growth of an individual and the maintenance of a healthy society.

1. STAGE OF THE LEARNER OR BRAHAMCHARYA ASHRAM – FORMATION OF SELF OR EGO

Brahamcharya doesn't mean celibacy. It means learning to walk the path of *Brahman* or the expansion of consciousness. If sex or other desires are an obstacle on the path then we must regulate them.

The Brahamcharya stage extends from the birth to the age of 25-30 years. Various brain researches indicate that the cognitive component of the brain that deals with reason, planning and the future matures by the age of 25 years. These first 25-30 years of life are spent in the following ways:

- Studying and mastering a set of skills in order to take one's place in the society as a self-reliant and confident individual who is able to earn a livelihood. A person can't become an adult without being financially independent. A healthy ego or self has four cardinal features: Self-care, Care of others, Trust and Boundaries.

- Becoming well versed in the philosophy and science of the cosmos, so that one can perceive the world and the universe as interconnected and interdependent.

- At the end of the stage of learner or Brahamcharya ashram, not only does a person develop a healthy ego but also realizes its limitations. A person becomes aware that the ego, although essential to live in the world and society, is an obstacle to living according to one's own nature. The path of life begins with the ego and moves into discovering one's soul or innate nature for healthy living and a wholesome life.

2. STAGE OF HOUSEHOLDER OR GRIHASTHA ASHRAM – MATURATION OF SELF

Grihastha means 'to be established in the home'. In this ashram, we take our place within a family and within the larger society. During this stage, our ego matures through the varied experiences of family life. This stage goes up to the age of 50-60 years or so. These 25-35 years are spent in doing the following:

- Fulfilling our needs for wealth and possessions (Arth) in an ethical way
- Fulfilling our desires for sex and other enjoyments (Kam) in an ethical way
- Fulfilling our duties towards our family and society (Dharma)
- Remaining aware of our ultimate goal of liberation (Moksha)

The fulfilment of natural desires in an ethical way is important, because if we go against our nature, we will be riddled with conflict. This will inevitably lead to an unhealthy life.

3. STAGE OF EXPLORER OR VANPRASHTHA ASHRAM – EXPANSION OF SELF

Vanprastha means 'leaving for the forest' which is a metaphor for exploring the unknown, or the higher reaches of life and consciousness. Vanprastha begins at the age of 50-60, when the householder stage is ending and the person is retiring from the job or work. This stage is particularly relevant to the people who are reaching retirement age. When we are in a job, we have to retire at some point to make place for younger people. Similarly, in the family we must step aside and allow the new generation to take on decision-making roles. When we were in service, business or trade, we were naturally expecting returns for services rendered or the capital invested. Now we need to free ourselves from this attitude of give and take. A Vanprasthi only gives and does not expect anything in return. It is a time for repaying the societal debt that one has incurred during first two ashrams. No doubt there is joy in the give and take of the earlier stages of life, but Vanprastha ashram offers a higher level of joy. When we give our service and our wealth with no strings attached, with little expectation, the joy we get is incomparable.

Expansion of the self is the essence of this stage of life. In Vanprastha ashram, we can expand our consciousness beyond our family and worldly aspirations and strive for higher consciousnesss. When we enter in this stage of life, having the proper attitude makes us "in the world" and yet "not of the world" at the same time. This attitude takes us beyond the limited attachments that we cultivated during the householder stage and brings freedom. This fresh expanded self includes not only our family and friends, but also the whole world. We become as vast as the universe. This brings us the experience of our own soul and universal consciousness.

4. STAGE OF TRANSCENDENCE OR SANYASA – TRANSCENDENCE OF SELF

Transcendence or Sanyasa is the last stage of life. During this stage, the arrow of consciousness is turned inward. *Sanyasa* means 'to integrate'. Sanyasa is not about leaving or renouncing anything. It is about integrating all that was experienced with the higher states of consciousness. Such integration paves the path to transcendence, leading to the experience of liberation or *Moksha*.

In Sanyasa we experience the boundless freedom of no-self or no-mind. Our sufferings come to an end and we achieve peace and prepare for the death of the body.

Chapter 8

EXPERIENCES ON THE PATH OF NATURALITY, PART 2: THE SOUL STATE

In the preceding chapter, we explored how the ego creates an image of the world around us, and of our place within that world. Although it has an important role to play in our lives, the ego also imposes limitations that affect our ability to understand ourselves.

As we begin to move beyond the confines of the ego, we become aware of a deeper source of knowledge. This is the knowledge of the soul. The word "soul" has been used in many different contexts, both secular and religious. Here I am using the word soul as a way to refer to our innate nature, which often remains hidden from our conscious perception. As we tap into soul knowledge, we move to a much more profound understanding of ourselves.

DISCOVERING OUR INNATE NATURE

Despite the limitations imposed by the ego, there is always a part of our being that does not surrender to these constraints. The flame of innate nature burns brightly deep within each of us, calling us to explore our own unique path. Our innate nature is dynamic and constantly sends signals of its presence. We may ignore it in order to maintain a comfortable existence within society, but then we live a fragmented life plagued by a persistent conflict between our innate nature and the ego. It is the struggle between what is and what should be.

This fragmented life can lead to a persistent state of alienation, conflict and discontent. We are aware that something is missing from our lives—something precious and unique. We lack a sense of wholeness and fulfillment, but we don't know how to achieve this state of well-being. As a result, we struggle with a deep sense of frustration. There are many ways in which we try to assuage that frustration, whether by the pursuit of material goods, power, or money.

In an earlier chapter, we explored the concept of innate nature at some length, drawing in concepts from Ayurvedic ideas about constitution and personality. As we progress on our inner journeys, we begin to reclaim our own innate nature. As this seed of self-understanding begins to grow and then to flower, we become increasingly aware of our own destiny—the unique roles that we are meant to play in this world.

But the path to discovering our innate nature is a long and difficult one. Teachers, parents and social and religious leaders encourage children to dream, wanting children to achieve great things to help create a better world. Rarely do adults encourage children to realize and express their innate and natural potential. These waking dreams become part of the ego. Although these dreams are borrowed from culture, we still carry them with us to escape fear. Such dreams don't come from a child's authentic nature, so they are fragile and can shatter easily when faced with the existential problems and challenges of life.

Children are encouraged to dream in order to reach the top of the social ladder. However, once the dream is realized, many still remain unfulfilled and the search goes on for more. It is rare to meet people who feel a sense of fulfillment and abundance after having achieved their dreams. These borrowed dreams cannot bring contentment.

But does this mean we should not have dreams at all? Dreams are both wonderful and appropriate if they are in accordance with our own nature and not against it. They can bring passion and joy. Once we are in touch with our true nature, a different kind of dream emerges. These dreams express our innate nature through the arts, science, religion and a new culture.

In the process of fulfilling our dreams, reaching a goal becomes the most important task. This becomes a burden because we want to attain the reward as soon as possible with the least amount of effort. But when dreams emerge from our inner nature then the journey becomes as delightful as the destination. Our parents, teachers, leaders or culture no longer determine our goals. We decide what goals to pursue and we feel fulfilled because both dream and action come from within. Each person comes to a point of self-actualization, and will experience the same joy of fulfillment regardless of their position.

However, this natural process is all too rare. Most of us pursue dreams contrary to the natural flow of life and inevitably, they are shattered. This disillusionment is painful but it opens the door for the discovery of our own nature. However, disillusionment in itself is not sufficient for true transformation. Disillusionment may temporarily shatter the worldview given to us by culture and give us a brief glimpse of who we truly are. Usually however, cultural traditions, family and religion swoop in to pacify us. Before we can go beyond disillusionment in search of our innate nature, we are seduced back into society. Since most of us cannot endure the pain of disillusionment, we happily accept the consolation of these old dreams and abandon our quest for truth.

A person who never pays attention to their own innate nature remains ignorant about the power and energy hidden within and depends on external sources for psychological survival. The path of self-discovery is not easy, since a new way of living has to replace the old. Everything truly new has to come from within the seeker rather than from the outside world. Often the disillusionment that brought about the possibility of self-discovery is quickly replaced by another dream from culture and the cycle starts all over again. The person never arrives at the state of self-fulfillment.

These dreams ultimately lead us nowhere. There is no progress on life's path, as we keep moving within the same boundaries. Slowly the inevitable physical and psychological decay sets in. As we grow old, both in body and mind, society leaves us behind. After a life spent pursuing dreams and goals shaped by culture, we are seemingly discarded. We become obsolete in the outer world and empty within. Stripped of outer rewards, we face old age in desolation.

However, we may refuse to accept dreams re-packaged by society. We say "no" to the prescriptions, distractions and consolations, and refuse to forget the wound that disillusionment has created. Rather than distracting ourselves in the pursuit of mindless pleasure, we can feel the pain in its entirety. We don't seek shelter in theories, philosophies or religion, but stay with what we are experiencing in its full depth and darkness. We refuse to repair the shattered dreams, because we realize that underneath lies something precious. As we allow ourselves to undergo this process, the sensitive self emerges. In the darkness of despair, a nascent self has been nourished. Without the death of the old self, the new cannot be born or grow. Despair is poison for the old self, but it is vital nourishment for the emerging natural self.

Despair is a time of darkness during which one does not know where to go. This is a difficult time because all that belongs to the past becomes futile and meaningless. Relatives, friends, power, wealth, religion—everything that once formed the foundation of life, feels empty and meaningless. Yet from this darkness, new life emerges. In the process of rebirth, we become psychologically free.

The journey from the borrowed dream into Soul is about the transformation of a person into an individual.

The most surprising thing is that after disillusionment, dreams return. These dreams, however, are rooted in our individuality and innate nature and contain all the energy and passion of our body, feelings and thoughts.

The process of shattering, disillusionment and rebirth into our innate nature is summarized below.

Normal endless cycle of life and death

Dreams (worldly)
Deeds
Disillusionment
Distractions and dreams
Decay
Death (physical)

Ending the endless cycle and moving into freedom

Dreams (worldly)
Deeds
Disillusionment
Despair
Death (psychological)
Deliverance
Dreams (innate)

SOULFULNESS: FULL FLOWERING OF THE PERSON

While the ego is the foundation of human life in the world, the soul roots us in our innate nature. Our home becomes internal rather than external. The soul is the flowering of a person and in soulfulness we become fully functional individuals. Like the ego, the soul expresses itself in many ways. Below are some of the main ways that we can feel the presence and movement of soul.

- Connection—love and compassion
- Natural meditation
- Well-being
- Healing and creativity
- Accepting mortality
- Awakening of our bodily, emotional and intellectual intelligence
- Witnessing consciousness
- Discovering destiny

CONNECTION: LOVE AND COMPASSION

The word soul comes from the word "solo" which means to "stand alone." However, it doesn't mean feeling lonely or living in isolation. Aloneness is the experience of being with one's own self. To be alone means that the inner space which was once occupied by the ego is emptied and refilled by one's own fullness.

With soulfulness there is a sense of space within to move, think and live. We don't feel isolated because now connection and communication with the world is genuine, authentic and wholesome. True compassion develops. In order to be compassionate we must have enough space within to truly feel another's fear and suffering. We can't be compassionate when our inner space is cluttered with our own sorrows and unresolved problems.

When we try to show compassion through an ego state we inevitably fail, because the ego is riddled with divisions and fragmentations. Our compassion is selective and biased. We constantly react to events, mostly based on unconscious biases and judgments as well as memories of past events. Reaction is always based on the past and future and creates chaos in the psyche, consuming a great deal of energy, reopening old wounds and creating new wounds. So much of the time we live a wounded life, due to this recurrent process of reaction.

However, the soul responds rather than reacts. A response is immediate, without any involvement of the past or future. Response is conscious and comes from the present moment. Mirroring, and the compassion that is born out of it, is a state of total perception without delay or analysis of any kind. It is not a thought-out process but an immediate response, not interfered with by memory. It's a complete feeling that doesn't leave a mark on the brain. The brain becomes a smooth, self-cleaning mirror.

Here we must make a distinction between compassion, sympathy and empathy. Sympathy is a cultivated pattern of words and gestures, taught to us in order to form relationships with others. Sympathy is a necessary social and cultural formality, but it doesn't touch the true heart. In contrast to sympathy, empathy comes from the heart and is authentic. One feels the pain and sorrow of another and is ready to extend a helping hand. But the problem with empathy is that we often accumulate the suffering of others and become burdened by them.

True compassion doesn't consume energy nor does it carry any notion of sacrifice. In true compassion, the person feels the sorrows and pain of the other, and responds. But those sorrows and pain don't leave any mark on the person. Everything is experienced and then it's gone. It emerges from within, without seeking recognition or reward, and is accompanied by joy and energy. One does not become depleted when offering true compassion, because it arises from an inexhaustible well within.

NATURAL MEDITATION

The ego's self-reflection and self-observation is incomplete because the ego cannot penetrate the subconscious. Its world remains divided and so ego meditation is a technique only and not natural meditation. While in a soul state, all is observed and reflected without judgment. It's like standing on the shores of a turbulent ocean and watching the waves with complete serenity. Meditation becomes effortless and spontaneous—natural meditation.

WELL-BEING

At this point, the social and cultural conditioning of the ego is shattered and the brain and body are freed from constriction and conformity. They are filled with energy. The reward or pleasure centres become fully active on their own, without stimulation from outside. The sense of well-being that arises doesn't depend on external factors, so we become less dependent on the world for pleasure, happiness and joy. This soul state has been described as being "intoxicated with the Divine." This state is also the experience of wholeness.

HEALING AND CREATIVITY

Compassionate, loving and non-judgmental witnessing of the world, both inside and out, is the beginning of healing. Such witnessing is free from anger, fear, disgust, guilt or shame. The flame of awareness illuminates the hidden subconscious mind, where old wounds, scars and painful memories have accumulated. These memories consume the precious resources of the brain, leaving little energy to face and resolve life's deeper problems. Awareness turns these memories into a stream of energy. This energy washes away the old from the brain and body, and old wounds are healed. We are left with a clear body and mind.

Soulful creativity is different from ordinary creativity. In ordinary creativity, new forms of poetry, science, music and philosophies are created. Although the soul's creativity includes all these creative expressions, it also helps in recreating the creative people themselves. With awareness and compassion, we are carved into new individuals. We are recreated according to our own innate nature and reborn as fully functional and healed individuals.

The lives of many creative people are full of suffering, discontent and self-destruction. Those around them also suffer and pay a high personal price. However, in soulful creativity, we are in harmony within ourselves and with the outside world.

AWAKENING OF BODY, EMOTIONAL AND INTELLECTUAL INTELLIGENCE

At the very root of individual existence is our innate nature. This nature branches into three components of our being: body, emotions and thoughts. Each has its own intelligence. The higher the position of a component in terms of evolution, the more powerful and dominant that component becomes. Emotion is more powerful than the body and the intellect is stronger than emotion. The ego muffles the intelligence of the body, which results in a conflict between the intellect, emotions and body.

As we discussed earlier, the pure direct experiences of the body and emotions are filtered and edited by the ego. We rarely experience anything directly, because of fear of the unknown. When the ego goes through the dark and turbulent passage of the subconscious, it is slowly stripped of its power. Only at this point is it possible for us to face our own death. In these moments of clarity, we realize that the notion of "I as the doer" is an illusion. As the illusion of the doer ends, witnessing consciousness begins.

Two stories from the ancient Hindu scriptures illustrate the significance of facing our fear of death. The *Katha Upanishad* is a book of rare beauty and depth, in which the story of Nachiketa captures the essence of the dialogue between life and death. Nachiketa is a young man who has a deep faith as well as an inquiring mind. One day he questions the meaning of a ritual that his father is performing. His father is insulted by his probing questions and curses him, sending him to face the Lord of Death, Yamraj. In a moment Nachiketa arrives at the abode of Yamraj, a place from which nobody ever returns to the world of the living. Yamraj is not at his home, and Nachiketa has to wait three days for him to return. When Yamraj finally returns, he becomes curious about this boy who has waited so long to see him, and has such an inquiring mind. After they speak for some time, Yamraj finally tells Nachiketa that he may return to the land of the living and that he will be granted three boons. For the third boon, Nachiketa asks: "Lord! Every living being in the world is mortal. They go through a cycle of happiness and grief in accordance with their meritorious work or sin. It is said that even if the body dies, the soul remains eternal. What is the secret of this? Tell me the answer to this."Yamraj wants to avoid the answer to this question but Nachiketa persists. Finally, Yamraj elaborates on the nature of the true Self, which persists beyond death. The key of the realization is that this Self (within each person) is inseparable from the supreme spirit, the vital force in the universe. Satisfied, Nachiketa returns to his home and re-unites with his father. The meaning of this story is that only the knowledge of death can bless us with a full life.

The same theme is explored in the story of Savitri and Satyavan, from the epic known as the *Mahabharat*. Savitri, representative of feminine energy, frees Satyavan, the masculine force, from death by her courageous encounter with the Lord of Death. Satyavan is a prince who is told by a seer that he will die at an early age. The princess Savitri loves him deeply, and marries him in spite of knowing about the prediction. Satyavan does die at his appointed day and time and is taken away by Yamraj, the Lord of Death. But Savitri has a determined spirit, and decides to follow Yamraj into the Kingdom of Death. Moved by her devotion, Yamraj finally agrees to restore Satyavan to life. The Savitri-Satyavan story is a metaphor about the meaning of life and death. Savitri in this story represents the embodiment of spirit and spirituality, which is capable of bringing the essence of life back from the clutches of death. Consciousness, rather than the physical body, is the essence of life.

THE BODY'S INTELLIGENCE:

We are grounded in our bodies, the basis of our lives. Within the body, all evolution and involution takes place. The last part of involution, the most difficult to achieve, is the expansion of the body's intelligence into a universal experience. This is discussed in the teachings of Sri Aurobindo, Mother and U. G. Krishnamurti, whose writing is referenced in the Appendix.

How can the expansion of the body's intelligence be described? Although we can be aware of thoughts and emotions, we are only dimly aware of the interior functioning of the body. It is a dense darkness where consciousness lies deeply buried. Most of us go through life never becoming aware of the body's unique intelligence.

In animals, the body moves and functions in instinctual patterns that govern eating, sleeping, and reproduction. But in humans, this bodily rhythm is disturbed by the ego. The quantity of food, exercise, sleep, sex, and work are all governed by the ego and this comes in direct conflict with the natural rhythm of the body.

When a person moves into a soul state, the ego's grip is released and the body begins to function with its natural rhythm, with an inherent inner discipline. It's a state of natural austerity, where the body takes what is necessary to maintain life, no more, no less. There is no withdrawal or indulgence. When the body is functioning with its own natural rhythm, it maintains an inner balance or homeostasis. In this state of homeostasis, we feel a deep sense of well-being and energy. A constant sense of well-being is a sign that the body's intelligence has awakened. This is an important step on the journey, but by no means the last.

EMOTIONAL INTELLIGENCE:

Emotions originate in the body and are connected to the limbic system of the mammalian complex of the brain. Emotions provide finely tuned input about the internal and external environment, which helps to protect the body and maintain a state of internal balance or homeostasis. While the body has its own mechanisms for maintaining balance, emotional intelligence compliments and enhances these mechanisms. Emotions are spontaneous and automatic. When we become conscious of them, we experience them as feelings. The distinction between emotions and feelings has been clearly described in the writings of neuropsychologist Antonio Damasio.

There are six primary emotions: fear, anger, happiness, sadness, surprise and disgust. These six have been observed in the facial expressions of people from various cultures all over the world. Out of these six emotions, four and a half are negative. Surprise can be negative and sometimes positive. We have more negative emotions to ensure survival against the many dangers present in the world. Fear is the most basic emotion and the root of all other emotions, as we have explored.

Many of the emotions and feelings we cherish are compound emotions created by social and cultural conditioning. They are a mix of primary emotion and social and cultural learning. Such emotions include guilt, jealousy, shame, resentment, love, hatred, and embarrassment. All emotions have their own purpose, even those that we typically classify as "negative" emotions. When the emotion is not connected to the body and the higher cognitive functions, then it can have detrimental effects. For example, fear is useful to a point but in excess, it paralyzes and constricts life. Anger is a defensive action, but excessive anger becomes violence. Jealousy is necessary because it protects a relationship and pushes us to be our best, but in excess, it is destructive. Guilt is corrective but excessive guilt is a prison.

If emotions become disconnected with the body and cognitive intelligence, they can result in an unstable state of disregulation and dysfunction. In contrast, the body in a state of positive homeostasis nourishes and grounds emotions, while cognitive intelligence fine-tunes them according to our natural, social and cultural environment.

Emotional intelligence is a dynamic state of body and mind. It has two main features:

1. Emotions are connected consciously with the body and with the cognitive or thinking mind.
2. They are expressed consciously and not accumulated in the brain and body as memories, so there is no pattern formation and addiction to them.

Emotional intelligence is essential in creating direct, deep and stable relationships with others as well as with ourselves. Self-love and love for others originate from emotional intelligence. Emotions should be expressed and released appropriately, otherwise they accumulate and may become the cause of physical and mental health problems.

INTELLECTUAL INTELLIGENCE:

Cognitive intelligence is the ability for thinking, moral reasoning, analysis and also reflection upon our own thoughts. Ordinarily we borrow and memorize the thoughts of others, which become our thinking and knowledge base. When we are cognitively intelligent, thinking comes from within and it is based on the intelligence of our own body and emotions. While the body's intelligence is expressed through sensation, and emotional intelligence through emotions and feelings, cognitive intelligence expresses itself through thoughts. These three modes of intelligence are three dimensions of the same reality. In combination, they form one's innate nature.

The uniqueness of cognitive intelligence lies in its clear logic, reasoning and its awareness of the vast amount of memory stored in the brain. When we use our cognitive intelligence, we can use memories of past experiences to help us make decisions about the future. Our conclusions are then based on evidence that may be subjective or objective. The full expression of morality and conscience occurs through our cognitive intelligence. Cognitive intelligence is also the beginning of the democratization of knowledge, which doesn't discriminate between color, race or socio-economic strata. The intellectual mind, history, science, systems, the rights of the living and non-living are all products of cognitive intelligence. Cognitive intelligence is self-reflective, which is why no automatic patterns of negative thoughts are formed.

WITNESSING CONSCIOUSNESS

The soul is the experience of a seamless conscious union of the reptilian, mammalian and human complexes of the brain. This brings the new quality of witnessing consciousness or mindfulness to our perception. Witnessing consciousness also becomes integrating consciousness, where the convergence and divergence of experiences happen. In this state, the body and mind are integrated so they function as one entity rather than as fragmented segments. The mind-body split is healed.

Witnessing is the property of mirror neurons in the brain. Although the animal brain also has the mirroring property, it is much less advanced than in humans. This capacity is the reason behind our growth and evolution. It is also responsible for empathy, as we attempt to read the thoughts and emotions of others. In ordinary experience, mirroring is also responsible for self-observation and self-reflection, although it is riddled with biases and prejudices.

In a soul state, the brain's mirroring capacity is fully activated, which results in clear and non-judgmental witnessing. The union of all parts of the brain releases electrical and chemical energy that flushes out some of our unwanted memories, wounds and scars. If the mind is not involved and our consciousness is in a pure mirroring state, we experience life in a waking dreamlike state.

We can link this state of witnessing awareness to our analysis of the chakras. When the seventh chakra is awakened, this is the point where we become witnesses of our own bodies, emotions and thoughts and of the surrounding world. This awareness is non-reactionary because it occurs in the present moment and is therefore unbiased by the past. We observe the inner and outer world without judgment. However, this doesn't mean that we no longer discriminate between right and wrong. Rather, it means that the process of discrimination flows directly from the practical needs of society. We will still try to protect society from harmful behaviour, as we are still in touch with the fifth chakra of systems and morals. Rules and laws are necessary to maintain harmony.

Events and feelings are experienced moment to moment, and then they are gone. We neither carry the burden of the past nor are we trapped by worries of the future.

If we are burdened by the guilt, anger, and grief of the past or are anxious about the future, we are unable to live joyfully in the present moment. In a witnessing state, we still plan for the future but don't get attached to those plans and dreams. They are no longer of central importance to our happiness. There is no place for disillusionment because we have already crossed through that at the sixth chakra. In a state of witnessing awareness, we are sensitive, responsive and we have a clear sense of "selfness" (as opposed to "self"). In selfness, others become a part of our sense of self. This self keeps on expanding.

Witnessing awareness is the beginning of spontaneous meditation, which continues effortlessly whether we are awake or asleep. An intentional meditation practice is no longer necessary, because life itself becomes a meditation. At this level, even an act of violence is meditation because the action is taken as a last resort in self-defence, and is done with compassion rather than with hatred.

The sun of non-judgmental witnessing burns intensely, illuminating everything that comes into its contact. That field of contact is vast and becomes even more so by the process of constantly breaking old boundaries and walking into unfamiliar territory, gaining new knowledge and insights about one's own self and the outside world. The external world is created by the mind, and when we understand the mind we know the world also. When our mind dies for a few moments and is born as pure self-awareness, the outer world also dies and is born anew. In this new state of awareness, both the inner and outer reality become one ground of truth, on which the ever-changing world of joy and sorrow rises and disappears like a wave in the ocean. The witness to this rise and fall of the world remains tranquil and unwavering.

ACCEPTING MORTALITY

Accepting our own mortality is the prime achievement of soulfulness. Here we are not referring to physical death but accepting the death of the ego. We can accept physical death but it is extremely difficult to accept the total annihilation of consciousness. No matter how much we grow and develop, we wish to continue to exist as someone, somewhere. Longing to continue forever is woven into the very fabric of who we are.

As we have explored throughout this book, the fear of dying is our core challenge. It begins around the age of three and haunts us until close to death. Death is then finally accepted and occurs peacefully. However, from the age of three until death, we deal with the fear of death by drowning ourselves in distraction. This helps to temper the fear—otherwise it would be difficult to live and cope with daily life. But in many, fear seeps in and causes many problems, ranging from anxiety, depression and stress to bodily illnesses. Life, already constricted, becomes even narrower because all of our reserve energy is being invested in the management of fear and anxiety.

Because of our conscious or subconscious fear of dying, we don't live life but rather cope with it. Coping is not living. Life and death are two sides of the same experience and if we deny one, we deny the other. Living fully means living with all the dangers that come with life. We must explore life according to our nature and dare to move forward to experience and live it fully. The most profound moment in life is when we are freed from the fear of death. At this point, all other fears and phobias slowly disappear as well. This doesn't mean that we never experience fear or sorrow. They will instead pass through us for a moment and will be gone without a trace in the next.

DISCOVERING DESTINY

Destiny is the feeling of a clear, conscious purpose in life that emerges from our innate nature. A sense of destiny fills life with passion and meaning. It is not a job or a duty; it's a movement that continues until death. It never ends because when we arrive at a certain point, another journey begins. It may or may not be useful to society and we may or may not receive rewards for it. Yet when we are on that journey, we do not need external rewards, because the experience of passion, meaning and well-being satisfy that desire for reward.

Destiny is not an intellectual or emotional concept—it is embedded in each cell of the body. Our social and cultural environment may help it to flower, but the seed of destiny already exists in our body and mind. Life's purpose is to discover this seed of destiny and allow it to grow into a full tree.

Destiny ignites passion and unites the mind and body in a harmonious whole. It's there all the time and continuously gives us insights. We are born with our destiny. If we believe in reincarnation or rebirth, then destiny is the continuation of the story of our past lives, threads of which we pick up in this life. If we don't believe in rebirth/reincarnation, then destiny lies in our genetic makeup. It's predetermined but has flexibility. It has definite roots but also wings; the roots are in our body and the lower part of the brain, while the wings are in the newest part of cerebrum where we interact with the society and culture.

The basic nature of our destiny is innate and comes from within, but its expressive form has immense freedom and is directly related to the environment in which we live. For example, if a person is destined to become a leader, that leadership role may take on different forms depending on where that person is born. He or she may become a family, tribal, business, spiritual, community or national leader.

Unfortunately, many of us never discover our destiny. We die still longing for passion, meaning and fulfillment in life, and we feel as if our work has been left unfinished. Fear is the reason behind this. Destiny is a step into the unknown and fear is the response to the unknown. In Indian tradition, the stage of *Vanprastha* ("going to the forest") is when we step into the unknown and find our destiny. The last stage of *Sanyasa* or renunciation ("all is put forth") is the complete fulfillment of that destiny.

Chapter 9

EXPERIENCES ON THE PATH OF NATURALITY, PART 3: REALIZATION OF THE UNIVERSAL

Over the ages, many seekers, saints and sages have written about the concept of liberation, often called enlightenment. It is usually described as an esoteric, mystical and supernatural process that cannot be explained in terms of nature, biology and science. Liberation is thought of beyond material existence, reason and analysis. It is a common notion that biology and spirituality, as well as science and the sacred, are entirely different domains of experience.

In this chapter, I will challenge this notion. By bringing biology and the body into a discourse about liberation, I'll explain that liberation is not supernatural, metaphysical or otherworldly. It is the unexplored part of our nature and is available to all of us, all the time, if we want to experience it. In the past, thunder and lightning were considered supernatural and created by gods. However, as we discovered their origin, they became very real parts of our natural experience. The same process has occurred with many diseases, including smallpox, epilepsy and various mental disorders. They were once thought to be the result of spirit possession, but the discovery of germs and an increased understanding of the brain made it clear that diseases were a part of nature.

If liberation is understood to be a part of nature, then pseudo-mysticism (emotional and sentimental) will disappear and essential mysticism will remain. Pseudo-mysticism breeds gurus, experts and specialists who claim to have special powers. While sincere and honest teachers point out the right path, the corrupt and dishonest seek power over people and ask them surrender their mind, body and wealth. It is important to separate emotional and sentimental mysticism from genuine mysticism. Emotional and sentimental mysticism are connected with the emotional component of the brain, while genuine mysticism emerges after the integration of various parts of the brain and body. In sentimental mysticism, we remain mired in emotional experiences, mistaking them for advanced states of consciousness. We remain prisoners of fear and sorrow.

The concept that liberation is a biological phenomenon that can be studied is not a new one. Buddha and Patanjali (founder of Asthang yoga) were two of the greatest sages in history. They described their experiences as inner quests based on reason, and they refused to believe in anything mystical or based solely on faith. They stated that spiritual experiences are a natural part of life and could be explored by anyone through systematic analysis and practice, much like a scientist investigates the laws of nature and the universe. They were spiritual scientists through and through.

All of us are liberated at some level—however, there are always more levels of liberation to experience. Abraham Maslow's self-actualization and Carl Jung's individuation are stages of liberation, as are Buddha's Nirvana and Raman Maharishi's abiding in the eternal non-dual Self. If we explore Sri Aurobindo's teachings and the experiences of Mother of Pondicherry and U. G. Krishnamurti, they describe an experience of liberation that is body- and matter-based. These teachers talk about divine materialism where matter itself becomes conscious.

Liberation is not a point but a process that begins even before we are born. From conception to becoming an adult, we go through the evolutionary stages of the universe's emergence from Nothingness. If we continue to search further and succeed, we will experience Nothingness itself and be released into its timeless and nameless womb, the source of all that exists.

During the process of liberation we become more and more conscious, bringing more awareness and knowledge. Eventually during this process of expansion, consciousness transcends knowledge and we come to persistently live in a state of non-knowing and yet we are fully aware. Non-knowing is the direct experience of existence without the aid of the thinking and reasoning mind.

In essence, liberation is an endless process with no point of final arrival. A problem develops when we think that our own or someone else's liberation is final and accept ourselves or someone else as the authority. When we proclaim ourselves gurus or become blind followers of some other self-proclaimed guru, the process of liberation stops. We may bask in reflected glory and feel elevated while the guru is alive. However, once the guru is gone our liberation also comes to an end. Instead of doing the hard work of learning, understanding, practicing and experiencing, we waste time waiting for something to happen.

Learning from a teacher who is not posing as an authority or guru is a good spiritual practice. Spirituality, like medicine, politics, economics or physics, can be taught by an accomplished teacher. But no teacher can make us creative or give liberation.

Liberation can be reached by many paths. We must turn to our knowledge of our own innate nature in order to decide which way to explore. For some seekers, the path of devotion (bhakti) will be the most natural way forward. For others, the path of reason and logic (gyan) will suit them best.

In the preceding chapter, I introduced the idea of soul or wholeness as the peak of individual evolution. Brain dormancy comes to an end, the mind and body work in unison and we become fully functional individuals. The consciousness of an individual is not conditioned by culture and society. The self-esteem of an individual comes from within and there is a constant feeling of well-being.

However, at this point we are still prisoners of individuality itself, which is determined by our genetic makeup. Living with one's soul is not enough. We must go beyond the limits of individuality to become truly free. The process of going beyond one's individuality is the beginning of Universal Mind or consciousness.

UNIVERSAL MIND: EXPERIENCE OF GOD

The soul is the ending of all known paths, but it is the beginning of another journey that has no clear guideposts. In order to arrive at soul, we must ascend to the seventh chakra through the lower six chakras. The seventh and last one is the soul point. There is no path beyond it—everything is veiled in mystery. We can't do much except to be vigilant and wait. Suddenly it may happen: we are thrown off the edge of our individuality and released into vast space brimming with experiences. This is the realm of universal mind or consciousness, which is named GOD by many religions.

The experience of Universal Mind unfolds in stages, described as follows: a sense of Oneness with the World; the God Experience; Universal Love; and Becoming Prayerful.

Universal Mind is an ever-changing sea of experience. It contains the shadows of all that has happened, is happening and will ever happen in the universe. It is a store of all the memory records of human experience, nature and the universe itself. It carries the past, the present and also the future. It has the micro and macro, subtle and gross, high and low. It is a churning ocean of creativity. The greatest musicians, poets, painters, scientists and intellectuals access the energy of this endless creative force and if they remain connected, their creativity is never exhausted.

Universal Mind contains darkness and light, evil and good, negative and positive. The Universal Mind is the God of all faith-based religions. God is the sum total of all experiences ever possible. The God of Universal Mind is half dark, full of death and destruction, and half light, brimming with life and vitality. If we only accept the light and life and reject the darkness and death, we miss the totality that is God.

The God of Universal Mind is the God of duality. We experience God but we remain separate. The relationship is of master and servant, lord and devotee and lover and beloved. Although Universal Mind is vast and feels infinite, it remains within the boundaries of space and time.

Universal Mind is the womb from which all myths are born. These myths are the common heritage of humanity. They contain archetypal images and figures and often appear in our dreams. During dreaming, when the censuring and controlling part of the ego is absent, we have access to the mythic and mystical world of the universal mind.

Universal Mind is not tranquil or still—to be in constant flux is in its very nature. It's the state of being but also the process of becoming. Universal Mind is also named *KalpTaru* or "wish-fulfilling tree," because it can fulfill any desire that is in accordance with our nature. There is a feeling of total trust and surrender, and we become channels of universal energy.

With the experience of Universal Mind we feel a sense of oneness with the world, and the world becomes the expression of the one God. The grace of God in the world brings the experience of universal love, a love that is not selective or limited. It embraces all as the creation of God. In Universal Mind, death and life become lover and beloved and can't be separated. This brings further freedom from the fear of death because we realize that there is no death, and that when our body dies, the spirit lives on in Universal Mind.

UNIVERSAL NO-MIND: EXPERIENCE OF EMPTINESS AND NON-DUALITY

When God, mystery, creator, creation, time and space are all emptied out, then only pure consciousness is left. This consciousness is without name, form, time or space. It is nothingness, the beginning of stillness, tranquility and silence. The brain has no ripples of thought and becomes a clean mirror, reflecting what goes on within and outside. In universal nothingness all events, states, thoughts and feelings are experienced as impermanent. Life moves and changes on its own without an absolute self or mover. All is experienced as one interconnected and interdependent web of life.

The experience of Universal No-mind and Nothingness includes the following: Stillness; Universal Compassion; Ending of Thoughts; Birth and Death become two sides of one experience.

Stillness and peace are the cardinal features of universal consciousness. Either there are no thoughts at all or they no longer affect us. Streams of thought may flow through the mind, yet we stand apart from the turbulence of the mind and live in serenity. There is no fear of death because birth and death are realized as two sides of the same reality.

However, this state is not a detached state. We become an intimate part of the web of life but are still free. From this connection and interdependence, a compassion that is free from suffering arises. We come to know the nature of the world and with this understanding we can connect with those who suffer but we don't suffer with them. We also experience a state of actionless action, in which action is taken but memory of that action is not formed because there is no mind to retain anything. Brain, body and mind become like a lotus petal on which the drops of sufferings are felt for a moment and then they are gone, leaving no mark on the lotus.

LIBERATION ILLUMINATED THROUGH THE CHAKRAS

In Chapter 4, we explored the awakening of the chakras as a way of describing the progressive expression of consciousness. Later, we used the chakras as a way to describe human evolution and the future of humanity. In the next section, we'll explore liberation as illuminated by the chakras.

We can view each chakra as representing progressively greater understandings of life and death, the central problem facing humanity. The chakras express the same energy, but in different forms. In the first chakra of the body, the process of living and dying occur simultaneously. But with evolution, life and death become two separate entities which are expressed in different chakras in different forms.

This may be best understood by studying the following table:

LIFE AND DEATH VIEWED THROUGH THE CHAKRAS

First chakra :	Death and life are one
Second chakra:	Life is sex and fertility and death is impotency and infertility
Third chakra:	Life is passion and death is anger
Fourth chakra:	Life is love and death is fear
Fifth chakra:	Life is creativity and death is blockage of the creativity
Sixth chakra:	Life is life and death is death and they confront each other
Seventh chakra:	Life and death accept each other and exist simultaneously

We can see how our understanding of liberation is deepened by this reflection on the chakras. The language of the chakras gives us a way to express this inner journey from the ordinary to the sacred, and then to a state beyond. We can also explore various form of yoga practice that deepens our understanding of the unique energy of each chakra.

In this journey through the chakras, there is no fixed endpoint. Even if one reaches the seventh chakra, where life and death accept each other, there is still more to explore and discover. The ascent through the chakras from the first to the seventh is only at the beginning of another journey. Once evolution of the expression of consciousness reaches its peak, then one can begin to descend down the chakras (involution). Carrying the flame of consciousness, we explore the chakras in the light of biology and the body, until we reach the first chakra where the energy is most dense and difficult to penetrate. Illumination of the first chakra has been called Material Non-Duality. Yet even this is not the end—the human journey of exploration must continue.

The journey towards union of the universal and the divine is represented in the following table:

THE EXPERIENCE OF EVOLUTION AND INVOLUTION AT DIFFERENT CHAKRAS

Chakra	Evolution (individual)	Involution (universal)
First chakra	Matter	Universal matter and quantum world (Padarth yoga)

Second chakra	Energy	Universal energy or Shakti (Shakti yoga)
Third chakra	Emotions	Karm yoga
Fourth chakra	Feelings	Bhakti yoga
Fifth chakra	Intellect	Gyan yoga
Sixth chakra	Insight	Cosmic form with death and life
Seventh chakra	Integration	

Ultimately, yoga is the state when the individual and the universal are in seamless union.

Chapter 10

CONCLUSION: THE NATURAL BEING

The journey of Naturality begins with the development of a healthy ego or self. A well-formed ego helps us care for ourselves and care for others. Also, a healthy sense of self allows us to trust others, while at the same time to maintain appropriate boundaries to keep us safe. All of these characteristics are essential for us to live in the world. But as we described in earlier chapters, there is much more to be discovered. Each of us possesses an innate nature, which is unique to us. If we are able to perceive and understand this aspect of ourselves, we will be able to fulfill our destiny in life. But in order to discover our innate nature, we must leave behind the ego that has been formed by culture.

Once we begin the journey into an existential realm, the ego's protective thoughts, concepts and dreams crumble. When the body is freed from the domination of the ego, it wakes from its slumber and begins to express and regulate itself through its innate nature. This brings with it the first experience of existential delight, which emerges from within, independent of any external agency. It's the first true celebration of the body.

At this point, we begin to live in a soul state. We tap into the intelligence of our body, emotion and mind, and our lives fall into an effortless rhythm. Meditation becomes a natural process that encompasses all our daily activities. We are able to act with love towards others, a love that does not exhaust or deplete us. We remain filled with energy and joy, which heals us of past wounds and traumas. A witnessing consciousness develops, and we are able to live in the world with serenity even when the world around us is in turmoil. Through the light of this witnessing consciousness, we are able to perceive our true destiny in life. In this way, our innate nature is able to fully flower.

Beyond the soul state, we enter into Universal Mind or the experience of God. Here there is an experience of oneness with all of creation. We feel a sense of universal love towards our fellow beings and to Nature itself. Our lives become prayerful, and we live fearlessly. Life as well as death becomes a part of our daily lives. There are no guideposts anymore, and no techniques we can use to take us farther on our journey. Without conscious effort, some people enter into the state of Universal No-mind or Nirvana. In this state of non-duality, the human being is emptied out and then filled with compassion. This is an experience of pure consciousness, beyond space and time.

Some seekers may experience another state, termed Material Non-Duality, in which each cell in the body becomes fully conscious. This is not a religious, spiritual or mystical experience. It is a biological state in which cellular peace is experienced. Explosive energy rushes through the brain and body and cleans the mind, leaving the organism functioning with its inner biological rhythm. The body is alive, the senses alert and attentive, and the brain is receptive, in communion with the biological universe.

From these points, involution begins. Involution is the discovery of our universal nature, when the individual is united with the universal. It happens at all levels, including the level of the body. The body's boundaries melt to include the endless biological world, to sense its natural rhythms and to celebrate them.

The individual now holds the flame of consciousness, discovered at the peak of evolution at the seventh chakra. Holding this flame, the individual descends into the depths of the body, biology and matter. The individual descends into the depths of darkness until the light of consciousness within the body, earth and universe is fully discovered. With the discovery of this light of consciousness in the body and matter, we become Natural beings or *Sahaja*.

WHAT IS THE EXPERIENCE OF THE NATURAL STATE?

At the stage of existential and integrative consciousness when evolution is reaching its peak, the body is slowly freed from the tyranny of the ego and begins expressing and regulating its inner life. In involution, the body comes to its full flowering and unites with the biological and material universe. The individual is transformed into a Natural Being, or Sahaja, and lives naturally, or with Sahajta. This natural state is not an intellectual, emotional, mystical, spiritual or God experience. It is a biological state in which the body becomes a part of material and biological nature and the universe.

Individual cells within the body are transformed, become conscious, are cleansed of thoughts and function at their optimum. Senses function independently of each other because there is no ego to bind them together. They come together only if some action is needed in the world, such as finding food, shelter, or communicating with others.

The Natural being experiences a high-energy state in which the body and brain function peacefully at their peak. When tired, the body goes into a deep, death-like sleep and recovers to function again in its natural high-energy state. It is neither a state of bliss nor of despair. In this state, the mind is active only when needed. It otherwise rests in peace without interfering with the body or brain. Biologically, a Natural being becomes both male and female. Sex, appetite, exercise and sleep are effortlessly self-governed.

Living in union with Nature makes living simple. Simplicity is not a religious, spiritual or mystical experience. It is a biological state in which cellular peace is experienced. The body is alive, the senses alert and attentive, and the brain is receptive. Living itself becomes simple because philosophies, science, arts, morals, religions and spirituality are no longer essential. Life exists for life's sake and without fear of the end. Life and death become one natural process.

NATURAL BEING (SAHAJA): THE BODY IS FULLY AWAKENED

This state is expressed in the following ways. The body becomes fully functional, with all senses and systems operating at their peak. The first and second centres of conscious energy are awakened, leading to an awakening of the body's cells, a transformation and liberation of the body. Changes in nature and the universe are felt in the body, which is in communion with biological nature as well as the material universe. The body of a Natural being is affected by everything that happens on this earth and beyond. The experience is primarily one of physical sensation rather than of feeling. In a Natural being, life and death become one.

But this is not the end of our own journey towards truth. Truth is boundless and so the journey continues . . . according to our nature.

"Sahajam, Sahajam, Sahajam Asti"
"(I affirm Naturality, Naturality, Naturality)"

APPENDIX

SEVEN ELEMENTS OF NATURALITY

1. NATURALITY MANTRA

Dharma Daham, Dharma Manas,
Dharma Buddhi-Atman

Right care to body, feelings, mind and soul.

Dharma Priya Jan, Dharma Serva Jan,
Dharma Desh, Dharma Dhara

*Right care to family, community,
country and the earth.*

Dharma Neham, Dharma Ekam,
Dharma Hee Gatisheelta

Let love, harmony and flow sustain right care.

Dharma Jeevan, Dharma Chetan,
Dharma Hee Ananda Param.

Let right care bring the bliss of conscious living.

Sahajam Asti Asti Asti

I affirm this, I affirm this, I affirm this

2. SEVEN INTERDEPENDENT FACTORS BEHIND HUMAN PROBLEMS

Emergence of self-awareness

Fear of living and dying

Formation of ego, to provide a sense of safety and immortality

Alienation, conflict and discontent

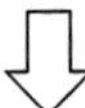

Decline in pleasure and well-being

Consumption of power, wealth, food, sex, drugs, knowledge for **pleasure**

Environmental destruction

3. THE GOAL: NATURAL LIVING OR SAHAJTA

Freedom from fear, conflict and discontent with experience of peace, passion and bliss

4. THE PATH: SEVEN DOORS TO NATURALITY

Choose one or many:

1. Natural Ethics: self-care and care for others
2. Self-Knowing: studying the book of life
3. Worship and Prayer
4. Fasting and Pilgrimage
5. Yoga Poses and Movements
6. Breathing Exercises
7. Meditation

5. CORE TEACHINGS

1. Innate nature (Prakarti)
2. Centers of conscious evolution and involution (Chakras)

6. NATURALITY PRACTICE

Practice for 45 minutes or longer:

- Twenty minutes for Bindu yoga, five poses: mountain, cat, prayer, bindu or marma, child . Ten minutes for breath of dissolution or Kalajayi breath

- Fifteen minutes for expansiveness or Braham meditation

7. EXPERIENCES ON THE PATH

- Ego: Knowledge of the World
- Soul: Knowledge of the Self
- Universal Mind: Experience of God
- Universal No-Mind: Experience of Emptiness and Non-duality
- Natural Humans or Naturals: U. G. Krishnamurti, Mother and Sri Aurobindo

ABOUT THE AUTHOR

Jivasu's teachings are called Naturality or *Sahajta*. Naturality is to "to live according to our nature" and "walk our own path." At their core, his teachings are about the fear of death (and life) and the emergence of the ego in response to that fear. The ego helps in escaping from the fear of death and promises an illusory immortality to its owner. This illusory immortality is needed in the beginning of life, but later on we have to go beyond ego to experience freedom from fear and true immortality.

Born in 1956, Jivasu (Pradeep Kumar) was trained as a pediatrician in India. He, with his wife Karen (one of his teachers), served for thirteen years in the remote villages of the Uttarakhand Himalayas. While living in Sivananda ashram he experienced his first awakening, which came to full fruition twelve years later in the experience of "wholeness" and freedom from the psychological fear of the death. Eventually the process culminated in the realization that death is not the end of life. The mind and the body die, but consciousness is immortal.

He conceived Expansiveness Meditation (*Braham Dhyan*) and the Breath of Dissolution (*Kalajayi Pranayam*), two elements of the Naturality teachings. He also concluded that all spiritual experiences have a biological basis. When the brain, the marvelous instrument of perception, is cleaned of memories and emotional scars, it will connect to and clearly reflect the universe within and around us.

Jivasu is the author of many books, including: *Meditation: A Path of Relaxation, Awareness and Expansion of Awareness, Science of Naturality, Chakras: The Wheels of Evolution and Involution, From Death to Immortality*, and *Offerings in Longing and Love.*

Currently, he teaches courses about Naturality (Sahajta) and freedom from fear of death and life in Canada, India and other countries.

Visit his website at: **www.naturalitypath.com**

CPSIA information can be obtained
at www.ICGtesting.com
Printed in the USA
LVOW12s1206290716
497982LV00002B/9/P